Praise for Farnoosh Brock and *The Serving Mindset*

"As an entrepreneur or business owner, the moment you learn to love selling is the moment your business transforms. Farnoosh Brock has created a powerful handbook for selling based on the only way that has ever truly worked. No gimmicks, no tricks, just pure service. Read this book. Apply it. And watch your business transform."

—Rich Litvin, Founder of 4PC and
bestselling coauthor of *The Prosperous Coach*

"The lessons here go beyond just what it means to flourish as an entrepreneur who sells. They go to the heart of what it means to live a generous, thriving life."

—Michael Bungay Stanier,
bestselling author of *The Coaching Habit*

"Believe in yourself, love your product, and introduce potential clients to an opportunity to make their life better. Radically different than chasing a sale, Farnoosh elegantly lays out how to elevate your business success by caring more, telling less."

—Dan Miller, *New York Times* bestselling author
of *48 Days to the Work You Love*

"I really wish I had read *The Serving Mindset* sooner. This is the type of book that makes my life better, and not just in business."

—Andres Valdes, Diplomat, speaker,
and author of *Leader by Choice*

"*The Serving Mindset* reminds me of its author: Smart, articulate, and wonderfully direct about exactly how to sell with love. My top takeaway is that raising your prices can be a profound act of generosity. I also love the idea that confidence is not a switch, but a ladder; this book will help you step up several rungs!"

—Caroline Garnet McGraw, Author, Speaker, Coach

"In *The Serving Mindset*, Farnoosh Brock guides readers through five mindset shifts essential for a growing business leader. She makes these shifts simple to understand and easy to implement, while demonstrating the value of continuous incremental improvement in each area. In return, Farnoosh asks only that her readers have an open mind and a willingness to learn and try something new. It's a refreshing approach to both business and life itself."

—Dominic Germana, Founder & Chief Engineer
at Impact Embedded

"If you love what you do but see selling as a necessary evil, *The Serving Mindset* is for you."

—Merrick Rosenberg, CEO of Take Flight Learning
and author of *The Chameleon*

"*The Serving Mindset* isn't just about selling, it's about how to view selling and business and even yourself in a whole new way that actually works. Farnoosh manages to break down so many beliefs and rebuild them with more useful ones, I found myself having a ton of 'aha!' moments about selling, my business, and even life in general. Selling truly is service. And it doesn't have to be sleazy or slimy. So, unless you're among the very few who are totally and completely comfortable selling their own work, you need to read this book. Now."

—Melody Fletcher, Author of *Deliberate Receiving*

"*The Serving Mindset* is a "must have" book for anyone in sales or coaching. Farnoosh Brock has written a book which resolves any seller's issues by removing the idea of selling from the equation, and then masterfully provides a solution that still results in sales. This is a book you will want to read, re-read, highlight, dog ear, take notes, study, memorize and recommend to all of your friends."

—James Halsey, President, Atlantic Benefits Corp.

"As a coach and entrepreneur, having confidence in my value and knowing how to sell myself is the lifeblood of my business. Farnoosh blends her wisdom, empathy and straight-talk to deliver a winning strategy for selling with more elegance and joy. *The Serving Mindset* will empower you to show up fully in your business and have people lining up to work with you. It's the book that I wish I'd had when I started my business."

—Michael Knouse, Founder of MSK International
and creator of The Council of Visionary Business Builders

"*The Serving Mindset* is a breath of fresh air and a gift to business owners and entrepreneurs . . . this brilliant book will leave you feeling empowered to take control, ready to elevate your business (and, most importantly, your clients) to a whole new level!"

—Bernadette Logue, *The Daily Positive*

"This is the first book I've encountered on mindsets that succeeds in applying them to a specific discipline that just so happens to be a struggle for many: Selling. But here's the thing: this struggle is a story you choose to believe. In *The Serving Mindset,* Farnoosh masterfully walks us through how to rewrite the stories we tell ourselves around selling, enabling us to grow our businesses beyond what we previously imagined."

—Jeff Brown, Creator and host of the Read to Lead Podcast

"Farnoosh nails it when she explains the difference between the scarcity mindset and the abundance mindset and how the former makes you want to sell while the latter enables you to serve with selling as a natural outcome! I loved *The Serving Mindset*, and can't wait to put it to use in my business."

—Margalit Grunberger, ACC, ICF Certified Coach

"Farnoosh shares transformational ideas that lead to a subtle but direct change in the way you feel about sales or selling. This book is full of practical questions and useful phrases to integrate serving into your professional AND personal environments. *The Serving Mindset* arms you with the tools and mindset to show up to each and every conversation and interaction as a true leader."

—Dan Sawyer, Senior Director at Fidelity

"Farnoosh extracts the timidity, fear, and lack of self-confidence business owners feel when having to "ask," truly allowing readers to change their unsuccessful mindset and grow into a new and positive method of thinking about sales. *The Serving Mindset* is a must read."

—Sharon Anita Hill, President,
Sharon Hill International

"Farnoosh taught me how to sell myself effectively. Her wisdom, insight, and mentoring skills are exceptional."

—Joy Sutton, Host of *The Joy Sutton Show*

"A potent combination of steely confidence and heart-centered empathy that translates well in industries of all stripes. . . . Farnoosh transforms [sales] from an ick-inducing, fear-filled chasm that must be crossed to the warm beating heart of a world-changing, mission-oriented enterprise."

—Amy Simpkins, CEO of muGrid

"Farnoosh gives everything she has to help you, whether she is coaching you through a new insight or giving you business advice on how to approach selling. . . . Simply trust that at the end of your time together, you will walk away with new self-knowledge and insight about your business, as well as just feeling happier."

—Dr. Molly Leavitt, DC,
Business Development Manager of OsteoStrong

"Farnoosh is a brilliant coach with a big heart and a 100% commitment to serving above all. . . . She walks her talk and articulates her ideas in a simple and practical way, and she does it by infusing fun and joy with success."

—Jason Goldberg, author of
Prison Break: Vanquish the Victim,
Own Your Obstacles, and Lead Your Life
and creator of The Business UNusual System

"Farnoosh has helped me appreciate and trust my team, shed much of my self-preservation stance, and focus on our real goal, which is serving powerfully."

—Patrick Reynolds, CEO and President of
CrossLink Consulting Firm

ALSO BY FARNOOSH BROCK

The Healthy Juicer's Bible

The Healthy Smoothie Bible

The Big Book of Healing Drinks (2019)

THE SERVING MINDSET

STOP SELLING AND GROW YOUR BUSINESS

FARNOOSH BROCK

WITH A FOREWORD BY
MICHAEL BUNGAY STANIER

Skyhorse Publishing

Skyhorse Publishing books may be purchased in bulk at special discounts for sales promotion, corporate gifts, fund-raising, or educational purposes. Special editions can also be created to specifications. For details, contact the Special Sales Department, Skyhorse Publishing, 307 West 36th Street, 11th Floor, New York, NY 10018 or info@skyhorsepublishing.com.

Visit our website at www.skyhorsepublishing.com.

10 9 8 7 6 5 4 3 2 1

Library of Congress Cataloging-in-Publication Data is available on file.

ISBN: 978-1-5107-4195-9
eBook: 978-1-5107-4196-6

Cover design by Qualcom Designs

Printed in the United States of America

CONTENTS

For my parents, Shiva and Farzin,
who brought me into the world
and gave me everything in the world.

FOREWORD

BY MICHAEL BUNGAY STANIER

THERE ARE TWO BOOKS that are foundational to the way I strive to show up in the world. One is Robert Greenleaf's *Servant Leadership*. Its subtitle is wonderful: *A Journey into the Nature of Legitimate Power & Greatness*. It argues that the goal of true leadership is to leave your people better than when you found them. It's a simple but difficult concept: it understands that the act of empowerment (and who's not up for empowerment?) is often the act of giving up power and control that you currently have (hmmm . . . that's a little more tricky!)

The second foundational book, *Servant Leadership*'s dance partner, is Adam Grant's *Give and Take: Why Helping Others Drives Our Success*. Grant says there are three roles that you can play in a relationship—giver, taker, and *quid pro quo* matcher—and asks which of these is the least and which is the most successful strategy. The least successful? The giver, the type that sacrifices it all for others and is left depleted and used-up. The most successful? (And spoiler alert here:) The giver. But this giver is different from the first one; this one knows how to be generous and how to act in service, and how to do all of that in a way that "protects the core" and stops short of depletion.

Now, this stuff is immediately gettable in theory, but hard in practice. After all, how do you find that sweet spot between service and success? As an entrepreneur, it can feel particularly difficult—it's so easy to give it all away, price yourself into poverty, and have your heart broken. It's also remarkably tempting to build walls, pull up the drawbridge, harden your heart, and forget that you went into business to be helpful, not just to extract money from customers.

At my company, Box of Crayons, we've tried to plot the best path by starting with our organizational values. In fact, two of our six values address the tension between "be of service" and "flourish."

One of those values is "Be Generous." This is not just about giving resources away; it's about assuming positive intent, seeing the best in our colleagues and our clients, and showing up with an abundant and full heart. The other value is "Nurture Adult-to-Adult Relationships." It says that, with a generous spirit, we need to show up with boundaries, we need to expect recompense for the value we provide, and we need to ask for what we want, even knowing that the answer might be "no." At Box of Crayons, we're constantly trying to figure out the right balance between these two values.

It's taken me the sixteen years since I founded the company to figure that out. (And honestly, probably longer than that.) (And, even more honestly, I probably still haven't got it all figured out. In fact, now I think about it, I definitely haven't got it all figured out.)

That's why you're lucky to be holding in your hands this new book by Farnoosh Brock. Farnoosh builds on the insights shared by Greenleaf and Grant, and says: Here's how you move from theory, via mindset, into behaviour change.

Now, to be blunt, success as an entrepreneur can be measured simply by success in sales. That's why this book *appears* to be about selling. And while it is full of practical advice on how to put service at the heart of sales so you can best help your clients and get paid fairly for that help, know also that you're being tricked a little: The lessons here go beyond just what it means to flourish as an entrepreneur who sells. They go to the heart of what it means to live a generous, thriving life.

Michael Bungay Stanier
Founder, Box of Crayons
Author of the *Wall Street Journal* best-seller *The Coaching Habit*

INTRODUCTION: DOES THIS APPLY TO YOU?

IS THIS YOU?

You are running a business. You are a founder, a small business owner, an entrepreneur, or the CEO of your company. You are really good at your craft, whether you coach people all over the world, speak for a living, offer an innovative technology at your startup, consult companies in your field of expertise, or provide IT services for your local community.

You are in business for yourself because you cannot help but be in business for yourself. Being an employee at a large corporation may have worked in the past, but today, your business gives you a sense of purpose and impact, along with an autonomy that you would not give up for anything.

Becoming a business owner or entrepreneur is a unique journey. Some fall into it naturally and find their way organically; others prefer a more methodical approach, which may call for an MBA, a written step-by-step business plan, and membership to a number of business forums and associations. But no matter which path you take or what business model you adopt, there is one inarguable universal truth:

A sustainable, profitable business must generate strong and consistent sales.

You know this about running a business, and you have no doubt done your part to learn sales and implement it in your business. You probably have processes and systems, strategies and techniques, and a plethora of sales and marketing tactics. Yet if you are not seeing strong and consistent sales in your business, lack of information is *not* your problem. All the sales information in the world cannot turn you into a sales master if you're missing the right set of beliefs and perspectives to bring your business vision to fruition.

The right set of beliefs and perspectives forms a mindset, and in this book, we talk mindset: we explore your thinking around selling, we question your assumptions, we challenge your beliefs, and with five essential mindset shifts, we show you how to adopt a mindset that not only eliminates the idea of sales (or selling) altogether as you know it, but also pours joy and profit into your business. We are also going to use the force of the higher truth to steer you back in the right direction, no matter how thorough your conditioning. We are going to bring every single belief and ideal you hold around sales into inquiry and see if it holds up or if it falls into pieces. We are going to understand exactly how to condition your mind to work *for* you, not *against* you, and we're going to dismantle the unnecessary barriers you've built so your business can grow without self-imposed limitations.

Until you regard sales from a place of genuine service, enthusiasm, and passion, no new information or sales tactics can elevate you to the levels of your original big dream when you first started your business. To get there, you need a new perspective, and to create that new way of thinking, you must first adopt a new paradigm, a new belief system, a brand-new mindset. We refer to this as the Abundant Sales Mindset, the belief that your opportunities for sales are rooted in abundance, rather than scarcity. We will cover this in more detail soon.

Sales: An Emotionally Charged Word

Sales: it's incredible how much emotion we associate with that one word. Unless you were trained in sales and marketing and have years of experience in the field, you may relate to the commonplace distaste for and aversion to sales.

Most of us dislike it. We would rather avoid it at all costs. We prefer to focus on any other part of the business. We escape it by focusing on marketing strategies or social media campaigns. When we can't sell, we use it as an excuse to get sympathy from others, "You know, our product is good, but it's just *so hard* to sell in this market!" We distance ourselves from sales by hiding behind closed office doors and laptop screens. We feel conflicted about it, yet we need it. We want to sell to stay in business, but we'd rather not be terribly involved in the process if we can help it.

When I first started my business, it became crystal clear that my own inner conflict around selling was the ultimate obstacle to a sustainable profitable business, *and* I was determined to overcome it. To be honest, what I learned in the process surprised and delighted me! Creating a sustainable profitable business became tangible after that.

As I applied my new approach to sales in my business, I also began sharing my new insight with clients. It worked for them, too. Selling had transformed to something else altogether, and for those among us who absolutely hated selling, this was good news. Crazy good news! And because this process is repeatable for any business, in this book, I tell you everything I learned on this journey so you can create your own sustainable profitable results without having to ever sell again.

You no doubt have a set of beliefs about success and achievement in life and those beliefs have served you well thus far. Perhaps you were an A+ student, a thriving employee, a respected expert in your field, or a successful professional. You may have subscribed to the typical "work hard and you shall succeed" motto as your primary mindset toward success. When you transitioned to being a business owner, you naturally brought over the same mindset, and you expected it to work just as well in your business, especially where sales is concerned.

Except that this motto does *not* apply to sales. Success in sales is *not* merely about working hard.

Most entrepreneurs and business owners start with a big dream to do work that goes beyond their individual selves, to make a difference, to bring great ideas to life, to enhance humanity in some way, to put their dent in the universe, and to leave behind a legacy. But the sad truth is that when the original dream dims as "reality" sets in, when they focus on the "failure rate" of most businesses, when they struggle with selling or commiserate with other struggling business owners, their idea of what was once possible gets smaller. They no longer love their business as much as they did at the start. They may even be ready to throw in the towel and go back to finding a job. As the combined struggle of running a business and the dislike around selling grow, their inspiration dips and their big dream now seems galaxies away.

The good news is that an old way of thinking created this problem, and a new way of thinking can solve it. Your mindset will be the determining factor for your failure or success and, with this book, you'll be able to find your way back to the original big dream, renew your inspiration, and see infinite possibilities again in your business as you adopt a more successful mindset about selling.

That's why you need to "empty your cup" before we begin. You need to park your ego at the door and come in with a beginner's mind. I request that you start this book with a frame of mind that says "I know nothing about selling. I am willing to learn something now."

If you can do this—which of course you can—and remind yourself to constantly come back to this frame of mind as you read chapter after chapter, you will experience the intended inner shifts in your belief system.

Little by little, you will see limitless possibilities emerge for anything you wish to achieve in your business.

You will realize that even your most ambitious dreams are possible with The Serving Mindset.

MY STORY

TODAY, I COACH AMAZING individuals and consult with businesses on how to elevate their levels of revenue, impact and joy without compromising on their values, health or lifestyle.

Back in 2008, however, I was an unhappy "successful" employee at Cisco, the Fortune 100 technology giant, and constantly looking for ways to fill my boredom. New challenges. New projects. New ideas. Anything to stretch my mind. I'd had a great career with plenty of success, travel, income, and freedom, but I was hungry for something else. I wasn't sure what exactly.

Thankfully, I stumbled into blogging and podcasting, a fun hobby that offered a creative channel to explore new avenues of possibility. Then, after a life-changing Blogworld conference in 2010 in Las Vegas that my husband, Andy, practically forced me to attend, I turned my hobby into a side-hustle. At the time, I could not have imagined leaving my six-figure cushy job for the sake of an idea, and yet that was exactly what happened six months after the conference: I resigned from the tech giant and became self-employed in April of 2011.

Eighteen months later, my husband quit his six-figure job at the same company to join the adventure. We've never once looked back!

I did not know this at the time, but what made this possible for me was *a shift in my mindset* at that conference in Vegas. This shift happened during one of the keynote speeches, in which I wondered to myself: "If that guy on stage can quit his job and do this full-time, why can't I?"

It was the craziest notion, but I decided to hear myself out. The corporate journey had long since run its course, and the scales had tipped without my realizing it: My comfort with the familiar was less important than my discomfort with uncertainty. And uncertainty was staring me in the face!

When you have a job, you often have a road map from management that guides you on your path to the desired results. You may or may not like it, but you are clear about what you need to do. When you go out on your own, there is no such road map and the path can feel uncertain without one. The only certainty I had at the time I resigned was that I would *never* work for someone else. The rest I had to figure out.

My husband, Andy, and I both come from electrical engineering backgrounds. We met and studied at Clemson University. After college, I moved on to a start-up briefly before joining Cisco while Andy spent five years at IBM before he came over to Cisco. Even though we had never owned our own business, I was fortunate to learn a variety of skills in my multiple functional roles at corporate, as well as from my many mentors and coaches, while Andy remained highly technical in his work. With our strong analytical and logical backgrounds, combined with my heavy focus on executive communications, career advancement, public speaking, leadership, and project management, we were able to establish a strong business foundation and close any gaps by developing new skills, no problem!

I learned how to become a coach, a speaker, and a writer, as well as how to create a personal brand with blogs, podcasts, books, and online programs and products. Andy learned how to set up business processes and systems, how to run our websites, and how to book complex international travels, all the while doing our accounting, client scheduling and invoicing. We felt pretty good about our division of labor.

But one thing remained elusive: no matter how much I taught myself about sales, whether it was selling my coaching packages or pricing my products and workshops or writing sales copy on my websites, I was not creating a consistent stream of clients or product sales. I would have some success and then a ton of rejections or a dead zone, and the clients I did have would stay a while and then leave, stating "price" or "tight budget" as a reason. I would get a lot of "I'd love to hire you, but . . ." and "Your packages are totally worth it, but . . ."

I felt stuck. Confused. Inadequate. Frustrated.

At the beginning of my coaching practice, nobody was willing to pay my prices, so I thought I was too expensive and needed to *reduce* my fees. Since I couldn't imagine charging any less, I started to resent the idea of coaching altogether. I did not yet know the biggest paradox that I would learn much later:

It is far easier to sell high-priced service packages than to sell low-priced hourly service rates.

It sounds impossible, but it's true. When you do this, you get higher-quality clients, you grow your experience and confidence, and you feel fulfilled.

But at the time, I did not know what my real problem was. I was tracing symptoms back to a problem that did not exist: charging too much and therefore, coming up with a quick "logical" solution of charging less. But that was impractical. Charging any less would have required me booking hundreds of clients per year in order to meet my revenue goals—a solution that was neither scalable nor palatable.

This "race to the bottom" happens when you price your products and services for less and less in order to beat your competitors and make your business more attractive. It is, by far, the least empowering strategy for a budding business owner. And I fell for it.

I started pricing my coaching for less and less and putting together tinier packages in hopes of selling them in volume. I couldn't figure out why the cheaper packages were *even* harder to sell. I joined mastermind groups, read every book on the shelf about small business growth, bought programs and products to help me, learned every "marketing strategy" to figure it out. Some of this information was somewhat useful but none of it solved the issue. More information, you see, was hardly my problem.

Then something very interesting happened. So, I belonged to a mastermind group at the time (a mastermind group, as you may know, is where a small group of three to five highly motivated people who share similar goals agree to meet on a regular basis to brainstorm new ideas, coach one other and be a source of inspiration for each other), and one of my mastermind partners, Jen Gresham, former Military Scientist and Moonshot Coach, went to a conference where she gained an incredible insight. At a round table, she was asked to share her top business struggle, so she told them how hard it was to sell her coaching services. Their response: "You are charging too little, Jen!" Her response was, as you might be able to guess, "Excuse me? I just said I'm not able to sell at these prices! How could I be charging too little?"

And that's when the light bulb went off for her: It is easier to sell bigger packages. It is easier to sell a $10,000 package than a $1,200 package. It is easier to sign a $40,000 contract than a $4,000 one. We didn't know it at the time, but this simple mindset shift would skyrocket both our coaching businesses in the coming years.

I know what you're thinking. It makes *no sense*. You don't believe me. You're right that it makes no sense in a quick, logical, black-and-white analysis. Yet we found—to our shock and delight—that it works. This was the first notion that reoriented our compass toward the core of the problem: We were indeed charging too little for the value we were promising. We were not lacking more information to solve our business struggle. We were, in fact, dealing with information overload. We were lacking the right mindset.

In time, this simple shift in my thinking opened a doorway to previously unimagined possibilities, but at first, I refused to believe it could be *that* simple. This was an unexpected insight. How could selling more expensive packages be easier than selling less expensive ones? How can people be more willing to buy when the price is much higher? How can they feel good about paying more? It was counterintuitive, but I wanted to explore this insight. I had to empty my cup and be a beginner. This prepared me to take in all the paradoxes and ironies that come with this mindset work.

Identifying the real problem in business, and life at large, is an invaluable skill—often, we don't even know the exact problem that is plaguing us. We feel a pain or frustration, we point to symptoms, we trace them back to a plausible root cause, we see what we want to see, and, in our rush to solve the perceived problem, we don't inquire further. After all, it's much more interesting to explore solutions than to ensure you've got the right problem in the first place.

My long technical training all my life had turned objective logic into my number-one go-to tool to solve every problem. What I learned from Jen's experience was that when it comes to human dynamics, the same sort of logic that applied in my engineering class does not serve me here. This is where a higher perspective helps you see more clearly. This higher perspective has its own logic below the surface.

Think about a time that you were stuck on a problem, having tried all obvious logical avenues to no avail, and the ultimate solution seemed counterintuitive at first. For me, this was the case when I first heard the advice "slow down to get ahead." It was counterintuitive; it went against pure logic. Logic would say you need to speed up to get ahead, but if you explore this higher perspective below the surface, the logic will appear. When you slow down, you prevent mistakes and catch oversights, and thus exercise efficiency with your time and energy, eliminating rework and other consequences of not getting it right the first time. As a result, you might just get ahead by slowing down rather than speeding up! A higher perspective may not jump out as immediately logical, and for that very reason, it asks you to look more closely for the unexpected insight hidden below the surface.

The higher perspective in my case was this: the right clients are happy and willing to pay a premium for the services of a professional, and that is the smartest way to build a sustainable and fulfilling professional services business.

Our logical and analytical minds had wanted to approach sales in the same manner that they had approached a technical problem or defended a master's thesis years ago, but since we had already tried that route and failed miserably, we were hungry enough to believe anything, and this new mindset came at the right time.

We'll explore this pricing paradox in more detail in Mindset Four of the book. For now, let us address your logical left brain, which is probably itching to take back control here! You see, you have to go *beyond* logic to take the leaps that you dream of taking in your sales. The way your left brain is used to understanding these things, a lot won't make sense at first, so you'll have to allow a deeper internal shift to manifest here. You might choose to bring logic and analysis along, but don't let them drive. Put them in the backseat, take away their decision-making power for now, and come into this mindset work with a beginner's mind.

THE PROBLEM IS IN YOUR THINKING

If you struggle with sales, your first question may be: What do I *do* differently? A helpful question would be: How do I *think* differently?

Let's start with how you think about sales today, because how you think about it has created your reality. Your thinking and your reality are intertwined. The former always creates the latter. If your thinking says sales is hard, guess what? It will be hard. If you fear getting rejected, you will see every "no" as a rejection, or, worse, you may avoid selling so much that you don't engage in any opportunity even to make it that far. If your thinking says "I'm not good at sales," you won't be able to get good at it. This line of thinking is very common among those who provide professional services, such as coaches, consultants, speakers, trainers, educators, workshop facilitators, and IT service providers. Since your thinking creates your reality, we need to bring that thinking under inquiry now.

HOW DO YOU *THINK* ABOUT SALES?

What is the first word that comes to mind when you hear the word "sales?" What is the first feeling that arises when you hear it?

In a survey of entrepreneurs and business owners, when I asked them this question, three D words—"discomfort," "distaste," and "difficult"—ranked highest. To their surprise, they did not know this until they uttered the words out loud. In fact, the top emotions most business owners and entrepreneurs associate with sales are:

- Fear, even terror
- Overwhelm
- Resentment
- Aversion
- Distaste
- Reluctance
- Disgust
- Dislike

And then, when asked what the solution might be, they shared a number of ideas, such as:

- "I need to be more confident."
- "I need to delegate the selling to someone else."
- "I need to do more marketing."
- "I need to get a new website."
- "I need to hire a salesperson."
- "I need to do, do, do. . . ."

Those may all be great ideas and, depending on your business model, they may well be worth exploring, but this is not the solution to the problem of "fixing" how you think about sales.

Your beliefs are what you hold to be true based upon the lens through which you view the world. You have acquired these beliefs in your upbringing and other life experiences, and they now paint you a picture of every situation. Based on that picture, you make certain decisions and take certain actions. If the same circumstance were presented to someone with different beliefs than you, they would see a different picture and thus make different decisions and take different actions. The situation itself is neutral, indifferent, label-less. The situation comes without a translation. Our beliefs do the translation for us.

It's extremely hard to create something that is out of alignment with your beliefs. It's like having your instruments set to point in one direction, while you wish to go in a different direction.

Example: If you want to feel good about sales, to be enthusiastic and excellent at it, but your beliefs view sales in a generally negative light, you are in a dichotomy with yourself. You want one thing but you believe another. No amount of motivation and persuasion will help you to move over to this desired view, because your beliefs and values are pulling you back, determined to sabotage your efforts, because, after all: Your beliefs are your truth, your reality. Until your beliefs align with your goals, what you want will remain out of reach.

This is why a well-intentioned business owner determined to learn sales and negotiation skills can attend dozens of seminars and workshops, read lots of books, and learn multiple sales strategies and techniques, but still not produce the sales she so craves in her business, because every time she goes out to implement a new sales strategy, her beliefs start playing in her mind.

While she is busy doing and doing because she has some twenty-seven tasks to complete, such as setting up sales copy on her website or scheduling a phone call with a prospect, she hears that annoying voice of doubt and skepticism at the back of her mind. Deep down, she knows she doesn't *really* believe any of this is going to work. Her beliefs will always sabotage her actions. All her efforts are no match for her inner dialogue. The voice in her mind is relentless: "Yes, I see you're trying to do all this, but remember, sales is difficult, you hate it, you've never been the selling type, and besides, you are an introvert! It probably won't work!"

You, too, may have done your due diligence around sales in your business, but are still not where you'd like to be. You can see how other entrepreneurs are creating results on a whole new scale, though they may not even be half as qualified, as educated, or as experienced as you. What in the world is their secret?

These were my burning questions when I attended a conference of expat entrepreneurs in Southeast Asia in 2014. I met people with a fraction of my experience and expertise in their fields who were commanding unbelievable prices for their services and felt confident beyond their years. I didn't look to them so much as role models in how they were running their businesses, but their mindset acted as yet another pivotal point in my thinking. Their self-evaluation of *their* services may have been inflated, sure, but god knows my opinion of my own services was hugely deflated.

And so the only thing blocking my similar success was my thinking. I was thinking too small, and I realized I was the only one who could change that thinking and as a result, change the course of my business.

We arrive to this point when we've had enough. When we are ready to be honest with ourselves. When we are fed up with our own excuses. When we are tired of our own complaining voice. Because that's when we realize we can *no longer* blame an illusory disadvantage like a late start, a certain upbringing, a personality "flaw" like being shy or introverted, or our educational experience—like being an engineer or an architect with no sales background—or any other factor outside of ourselves.

The great news is that we—our personalities, our likes and dislikes, our deepest selves—are not the problem. The problem is inside our head, as is the solution. The work here is all internal and on this journey of mindset exploration and adjustment, we experience internal breakthroughs. We grow as an individual first, and then as a business owner, to higher levels of self-awareness and self-understanding.

WHY WE HATE SALES SO MUCH

Based on what I just shared, you may agree that most of us do have a generally negative viewpoint on sales. What's more, more than a few of us just flat out hate sales. We've even grown hyper-aware of it. We can smell a sales pitch a mile away and, as uncomfortable as it feels to be pitched to, it's worse yet to be the one doing the pitching because selling, for most of us, falls on the low end of the spectrum of intellectual work. We think we have far more important work to do than selling, like managing our people, setting up new services, doing more marketing, or optimizing our processes.

Yet, none of us can argue the non-negotiable value of strong sales in our businesses, so why such a negative viewpoint on something that is the lifeline of our business? Why do we hate sales so much? There are many theories out there. Here are a few of mine:

Case Scenario One:
Your Education or Corporate Job Did It to You

Confession Time: In electrical engineering school at Clemson, my classmates and I would ridicule the sales and marketing majors. Their coursework was so easy they could party several nights a week. We thought their major was a joke, and their future prospects would be average at best. If only they had to sit through one of our random signals theory or electromagnetic classes, they'd never survive. They'd never have the brilliant intellect it takes to figure it out. "You have to be smart to go through engineering school," we would say, sneering at them, "and mediocre at best to get a sales or marketing degree."

Ah, the naiveté of youth!

Fast forward to the corporate world, where I could still detect this mentality in my peers and myself, affirming that this type of ridicule was not limited to the in-group ignorance of our engineering school culture. There was a notable difference, though; if the ridicule came in giant waves back in college, now it had reduced to small ripples, but alas, it was still there.

My techie peers would constantly complain about how we always saved the day by solving complex problems, troubleshooting massive issues, and fixing underlying hardware and software issues so our customers could have all the functionality and usability they had paid for, yet we got none of the glory in return—that was reserved for the sales guys (and gals!). It was obvious that *we* were the true engines keeping this giant operation in motion, that we were the truly essential part, and yet "those sales guys" made the big commissions, looked great in front of customers, and continued to lie and finagle their way to the next sale by overpromising and underdelivering.

So it seemed the story had shifted in their favor; years later, those with "a joke of a major" were earning a lot more money and enjoying the sexy part of the business, too. Everyone knows about the sales parties, the enormous sales bonuses, the schmoozing-the-customer dinners and activities, and the privilege of attending countless trade shows and conferences and business trips and so on.

In my conversation with Greg Thomas, Founder of BetaRover Inc., he shared how the developers under his management shied away from any tasks that were considered to be "salesy" in nature. They had huge resistance to getting involved in the sales part of the process and wanted exclusively to keep with the technical side. These developers saw themselves in clean and well-defined boxes: I am a developer; I am a coder; I'm the person behind the computer. In their words, "Sales is not who I am or what I do! That's not my job!" The idea of sales was so fraught with negative emotion that they wanted to separate themselves from it and any suggestion of getting them involved in the sales process would always be rejected. To get them even remotely interested in any aspect of the process, even one as benign as providing a product training session for customers, Greg would have to get creative and find ways to position sales as a beneficial skill for any person to have.

As we the "techies" gain experience in the real world, our warped viewpoint of sales shifts from generally negative to one of mild resentment. You can talk to any first-line manager at a tech company and they will tell you about the tension between engineering and sales. Engineers have the reputation of advocating for the customer and being the "honest" voice about the capabilities of the company's products and services, whereas the sales guys and gals have a singular agenda: to close. This polarity of priorities feeds the resentment toward sales, a position that's easy to take when you are an engineer or a technical expert working in a large company—your neck is not on the line if the sales numbers drop, at least not directly or immediately. Because of this, in large corporations, if you are not in sales, you can afford some mild resentment about sales.

But now imagine an engineer with mild sales resentment who decides to leave his employer and start his own business. He's going to show the world how it's done, and how smart and resourceful he is, and he will get to keep all the sales commissions, too. How do you suppose his current mindset serves him when as a business owner, he will be 100% responsible for sales?

This is how a sense of elitism can fill your head with foolish thoughts and an inflated ego. Yes, electrical engineering—or any other engineering or highly technical field of work—can be a bloody hard major. Yet that in no way *diminishes* the immense challenge and value of sales in business, and this hypothetical engineer and all others like him have much to learn before they can create their dream businesses.

Case Scenario Two:
The Entertainment World or the Media Did It to You

The used-car salesman analogy never fails to make us cringe. Nobody wants to be THAT person: friendly but needy, possibly creepy, lying to your face, cheating you out of a good deal, making you part with your hard-earned cash, and harboring a guilty conscience (if they have one at all).

The entertainment world certainly does not glorify the role of a salesperson. We glorify the underdog, the struggling artist, the victims of society, and the humble people who give everything away and never want for themselves. Money is the "root of all evil," while compassion, honesty, and happiness are on the opposite side of that illusory dichotomy. You are taught to believe that they cannot co-exist. You cannot have it all; you must choose "good or evil."

It's very black and white, and it brainwashes you to judge the world with massive generalizations. It may seem as if your mind hasn't been affected by the media, but that is almost impossible unless you grew up in a protected cave away from society. You and I and everyone else are inadvertently affected by the strong cultural conditioning around sales. It takes a deliberate choice, combined with mental reconditioning, to reset your preconceived notions of selling and sales. You have to hold your every assumption up to light and see if it has any truth at all in the real world where you are growing your venture, selling your services, and planning to make a difference.

Case Scenario Three:
Your Parents or Family Did It to You

I'm going to make a bet here: No parent ever encouraged a child who said, "I am going to grow up to be a salesperson!" You were encouraged to choose a career that sounded honest and respectable, that put your talents and gifts and strengths to good use, and that made your parents proud to tell other parents. And yet, no career would ever exist if you could not sell yourself to your first boss, and no business would ever work if you could not sell yourself to your first customer.

Sales is the hidden essential machine behind every successful venture, operation, and establishment. Even a non-profit has to sell itself to its sponsors and donors and fund-raisers. Sales is inescapable in business. Maybe your family taught you positive values about business and sales. But what if your family glorified education, recognition, awards, sports, and arts, but nurtured a mild dislike or downright distaste for business and sales? Even if you never sat down and discussed the topic openly with Mom and Dad, your subconscious will have picked up messages along the way and made up stories that continue to affect your decisions and actions today to some degree.

If you are running your own business today, what you need more than anything—more than your parents' approval and more than academic accolades—is strong, consistent sales. If your subconscious is still hostage to this negative association that you innocently picked up at the dinner table or in the living room of your childhood, you need to recondition it now.

Case Scenario Four:
Spammers, Scammers, Unwanted Solicitors Did It to You

How unsavory can you get and how low can you stoop to become a spammer? To scam honest people with lies and deception? To go where you are clearly unwanted and then proceed to pitch your questionable product?

It used to be contained to the random solicitor call at dinnertime on the family phone. Now it's every minute, everywhere you turn, every social media platform, and every email address—nowhere is a safe haven from spammers. All day and night, you are being "sold sold sold," and if you feel disgusted by the concept of sales as you relate it to *this* experience, nobody can blame you, because THIS way of selling is very disgusting.

You may not see how this relates to your business, because you, after all, are never going to be a spammer or scammer or an unwanted solicitor. Agreed, but the association of these dirtbags with the grander concept of sales is already well formed in your head, and paints the whole idea in a negative light. Your subconscious relates one thing to the other, and when you are thinking and planning and evaluating sales in your own business, this association may cloud your vision. You need to clear it. You need to de-couple sales from anything unsavory.

Time for Re-Conditioning Your Mind

That is a whole lot of conditioning from many different sources, and you may have been exposed to more than one of them. No wonder you may not like sales all that much.

As a result of all this conditioning, a perspective is formed and nurtured over the course of your entire life, but is it true? When was the last time you stopped and asked: I wonder if my view on sales is factually accurate? I wonder if I can prove it? I wonder if I should examine my beliefs? Probably never. That's not how our human mind works. The human mind is proud of its beliefs and opinions and it strives to be right. So normally, we defend our beliefs; we stand up for our ideals even if those beliefs and ideals work against our higher interests. Our value system is a strong force in our life unless a *greater force* disrupts the system and forces us to see things in a new light.

BUT FIRST WE HAVE TO DECIDE

THAT'S RIGHT. YOU HAVE to decide what kind of business owner or entrepreneur you intend to be.

The Decision—that crystal-clear moment where your mind goes from saying "I'm going to *TRY* this mindset stuff!" to "I am *DOING* this!" This Decision is a point of clarity and it is empowering. When you decide, you call forth your highest self, you gather all your troops, and you are ready to set out and conquer whatever lies ahead. You are no longer wafting between trial and error, yes and no, maybe and maybe not. You're done exploring an idea and seeing if it will work for you. You are *doing* it. Exactly as Yoda preached: "Do or do not, there is no try."

You know this moment well. You've been there thousands of times in your life, even if you haven't been conscious of it. You decided by saying yes to your spouse or a partnership or a proposal. You decided to go on a trip, take a chance with your business, live in a new place, take a vacation, quit your job, or sell your stock options. In every case, a clear, made-up mind is half the journey.

Few things stand in the way of a made-up mind. Honestly, this should be the prerequisite to any self-improvement plan in life, and it is ours before the coming mindset work. The skeptic in you may want to first see data, proof, case studies, before you decide to commit to this "mindset stuff." That's fine, but if so, please know this: you won't see many statistics or data points or case studies in this book. Those books put me to sleep.

Instead, you'll read about real stories, real human dynamics, real transformations and breakthroughs that my clients, peers, and I have experienced over and over again. You'll hear me talking to you and taking a deep interest in you, your mind, and your freedom from the struggle around selling. If you share this deep interest, then we'll get along just fine.

The Left Brain Needs the Right Brain, Too

This shift in mindset is not an entirely rational one. That's what makes it both super simple and crazy hard to grasp. As we get into the limiting beliefs that have likely held you back, you will notice that you may have to put the logical, sequential, rational side of your brain—the left brain—in check and begin to engage the holistic, intuitive, imaginative, and visual side of your brain—the right brain. In other words, we need to use our whole brain in order to make these internal shifts.

But just how do you do that?

If, like me, you've primarily used your left brain to make (presumably) rational decisions and clear logical choices in your life, you will likely feel some resistance to quieting the logic machine from running constantly. After all, you have built a lifetime of habits to look at everything from a logical and rational perspective: You rely on logic. You rely on rationale. You rely on analytical thinking and clinical considerations of matters before you. You choose facts over feelings, linear thinking over holistic thinking. You may regard imagination, intuition, and feelings as "nice to have," but certainly not leading the way into your next phase of business success.

Yep, me too! As a trained electrical engineer with a bachelor of science, a master of science, a thesis in the field, which I proudly defended, and a CCIE certification (I nearly killed myself for that one!), I couldn't have been more reliant on my left brain to lead me in the right direction. Until at some point, the left brain alone could not provide the answers I needed for my life's next phase.

In fact, looking back at my life's best decisions, I made them with a deep sense of intuition, imagination, trust, faith, love, and alignment to primary feelings. When I resigned from a successful, thriving career at Cisco, I was not following logic. My family made a point of often reminding me of this. Yet, that "irrational, illogical" decision turned out to be the second-best decision of my life. (The first was to marry my husband!)

When I chose to invest in a business coach for almost two years at rates that, at the time, felt astronomical, my left brain argued constantly as to why this was unnecessary, how it did not make financial sense, and how I should figure it all out on my own. I didn't listen. I knew in my gut that I needed to take a drastically different approach in order to enable the drastically different outcomes I wanted.

I was right. And, moving forward in life, I've made every major decision since with both sides of my brain, so to speak.

Look, this is not to say throw caution to the wind, tune in your rock & roll music, drive down the road with the top down, and let your mood call all the shots. There is a balance, a mid-point, a place where your Left Brain and Right Brain can work together to call on your highest self and to empower you to bring forth your greatest answers. Those answers don't come from the left or the right side of your brain alone; they come from the whole brain.

So, are you ready to decide with your whole brain? Are you willing to enter the mind of a beginner, to become receptive to ideas that may be counterintuitive, and to explore them for yourself before you judge their validity? Are you willing to allow old habits to be set aside so that you make space for new ways of thinking about sales and your business? Are you completely invested in the possibilities that you can unleash by opening yourself up to a new paradigm?

If you enter the mindset arena in this fashion, you will meet much success along the way.

THE PREMISE OF THIS BOOK

CAN YOU HEAR THE HEARTBEAT OF YOUR BUSINESS?

Sales is the heartbeat of a sustainable, successful business. Period. End of story.

Lots of things matter in a business: the people, the culture, the product, the values, the website, the systems and processes. But how much do they matter? Not as much as your sales! You can stay in business if any of these areas is lacking or needs work. You *cannot* stay in business without selling. Sales is non-negotiable because, as I said, sales is your heartbeat. If your heartbeat is healthy and strong, it pulses growth, wealth, and longevity into your enterprise. If it's slow and constricted, your business struggles. And if it stops, your business dies.

This is the foundation of a business that thrives: consistent and strong sales. Notice I said "thrives," not "survives." You can survive on very little. And you can do that while hating sales all day long.

But if you're here, you are not interested in just surviving. You want to thrive and prosper and create a lasting impact for others with your business. Surviving is just about you and your immediate needs; thriving is about your impact on others as you fulfill a bigger vision. To achieve that, your sales must be both strong and consistent. If you have consistent sales in small quantities or strong sales once in a while, you're on your way, yes, but it is the *combined power* of consistency and strength in your sales over the long haul that enables you to thrive.

Your Thinking Determines Your Selling

Your thinking directly impacts your selling. Whatever your business model, the *right* sales mindset can result in transformational leaps in growth, revenue, impact and fulfillment. Your business model is actually irrelevant—you could be a carpenter, a coach, a speaker, a consulting firm, or a coffee shop owner; a healthy sales mindset, which I call the Abundant Sales Mindset, is the non-negotiable here. If you are in business to make a difference and create wealth and prosperity for you, your immediate circle (family, employees), and beyond, you should know that you can't do all this while harboring an inner conflict around selling. An increase in business acumen can only take you so far, and an MBA can only provide so many answers if, at the end of the day, the way you feel about sales remains in conflict with your highest purpose and vision.

Again, your thinking directly impacts your selling. So how do you know if you have the right thinking about selling? Easy: it feels good. You're running your business in a way that feels good, your actions line up with your core values, your decisions honor your vision and mission, and you are excited about selling because you no longer even see it as selling. You are gladly offering your contribution to the world and doing your life's work. Your inner conflict has dissolved into a joy and a confidence and a deep satisfaction.

That said, if you don't have the right thinking, you can change it. In order to tap into the power of changing your belief system, you must first be aware of the influence of ego in your thinking and then be willing to explore what you call "truth" or "facts." As long as your desire for a thriving business is stronger than your desire to stay in the comfort of your familiar-but-limited belief system, you're on the right track. You can do this. Internal shifts will happen.

Your ego, that loud, annoying, know-it-all voice in your head, wants you to fixate on your current belief system, because your ego survives and thrives on being right. For instance, if you insist to yourself, "I can't sell, and that's a fact!" your ego will want to defend that. The longer you've believed this, the deeper your defensiveness around it. Even if it'd be in your favor to be totally wrong, the desire to be right is stronger. That's why people get such a thrill from being right even about bad news such as the stock market crashing or friends splitting up. They love to say: "I told you this would happen! I knew it!"

(If the subject of fascination with being right and wrong interests you, I highly recommend Kathryn Schulz's book *Being Wrong*.)

Given that your ego loves to be right, it takes objectivity to step back and inquire into your beliefs by asking, "What do I really believe about myself and selling?" followed by "I'm curious if that belief is really true or helpful." It's delicate business to question our thoughts and put our ego in its place. We feel safe and comfortable with our current belief system. This is familiar territory. We've done things a certain way for a long time. We feel ambivalent about anything that falls outside of our framework of what is true.

But that's precisely where we need to go if we want to change our thinking: outside, in the unfamiliar zone, to find our new way home.

If your familiar territory has harbored your negativity around sales, it's time to abandon it now. If you're wondering, "OK, OK, but can I be just a wee bit negative? Can I hate selling just a little bit?" My answer is, unequivocally, "No. No, you cannot. Not if you want to create the results of limitless possibility for yourself. We are not negotiating on this."

A while ago, one of my role models called me out on my own hang-ups around selling. She had challenged me to raise my coaching package prices, not by a small margin, but by doubling them overnight. She could tell that while I was desperate to charge more and fully determined to rise to her challenge, I secretly hated doing it just a little. That little bit of hate made it SO HARD to do this.

My reasons were logical: I felt guilty for ruling out prospects who could not afford me, and for being so "daring" with my prices.

This led to a very important lesson: there is no way I can powerfully serve my clients if I haven't yet served myself. Whenever I harbored *even an ounce of* negative emotion or inner conflict about my prices, it impacted the way I showed up and served them. Whenever I felt even an ounce of resentment, it limited the magic I could create with them. So it was clear that I had to let that last bit of hate go if I were to maximize the possibilities here. I did this by committing to myself that *either* I will charge prices that feel right and then deliver my absolute best, or I will not take on the job because, make no mistake about it, negative emotion is poison for the mind.

Think of it this way. If you knew that there was one tiny drop of poison in a cup of water, would you willingly want to drink it? Now, if the water is your business, your hate for selling is the poison. So, you see, you can't be even *a little negative* about selling. You can't hate selling *just a little.* It won't work. Your water will be poisoned. You must eliminate the hate altogether. As you do, the joy in selling will emerge. Discovering that joy is the greatest surprise in all this mindset work. Now, let's discover this joy for you!

The Dilemma of the Technical Professional

I'd like to use the example from my previous world for us: the world of technical professionals. Most such professionals at one point or another reach a plateau in their corporate roles and come to a crossroads. Some go into people management. Some do nothing about it and lose passion in their careers, but continue on. Many move companies or join start-ups. A small number venture out on their own. This particular group sees their technical expertise as a unique asset that got them so far in their careers but couldn't get them much further, so they decide to start their own business.

But, as they contemplate the ideas of going solo, they face an invisible dilemma. You see, the average technical professional is passionate about technology, and whether it's obvious or not to him or her, he's far more interested in protecting his technical savvy than in doing what would best serve him in the business in the long-term. He may be ambitious, yet he lacks the full vision that running a successful business requires of him. This vision is often blocked by a blind loyalty to "staying purely technical."

When technical expertise is what you hold in the highest regard, all else concerning a business is immediately of lesser value in your current view. You might even have little enthusiasm in the overall extent of running a thriving business, lest you betray the spirit of your inner techie. I've known so many brilliant engineers and technical geniuses who could not get on board with the other hats they needed to wear—selling in particular—in order to bring their unique assets to the market. They wanted to set up everything in a hurry, delegate as much as possible, and go back to being a technical expert. It's very hard to do that without an established stream of customers and clients, and to acquire that, you need to step outside of your techie self and inside the human side of things.

THE MISSING PIECE

Imagine Josh, a fictional name for a person from a real story of the technical world. He comes from the employee world, where his role was more or less spelled out for him. He had certain technical skills plus two or three specializations. They called him a Subject Matter Expert (SME for short) in the corporate world.

One day, Josh decides that he wants to be his own boss. He decides to transfer his invaluable technical skills over to his own business in order to offer consulting services to his employer's competitors in the marketplace. Josh knows that he needs more than just technical skills to run a business. He's heard his techie friends talk about getting an MBA to learn management, leadership, and business acumen. He badly wants to succeed in this business, because he really doesn't want to go back to his old job, so he enrolls in an expensive MBA program. He does really well. As an A student in engineering school, an MBA program is nothing for him. He likes the material and he begins to see himself as an "expert" on sales and marketing, leadership and communications, and so on. He has to make a lot of sacrifices to make all this happen; he has to do his best on his fledgling business during the day to make ends meet and tend to his MBA work in the evening, plus pay for all this additional education. But Josh is persistent. After two years, he is an MBA graduate and has completed dozens of other courses, books, and programs on the non-technical side of running a business.

Now he has to apply his invaluable training to his business. It's time to integrate the strategies and systems and processes from the MBA classroom into his service offerings. It's time to use his new skills to showcase himself as a great asset in his market. Things are working well, and even if he has not yet replaced his old salary, he believes it's only a matter of time. This is all a dream come true for Josh.

A few years go by like this, and now, Josh is feeling exhausted from what he calls the "hard part" of his business: the selling. He feels the weight of doing the selling, even though he knows how to do it. He has streamlined his processes and has solid systems in place, but selling is not his favorite activity. Secretly, he wishes he could do away with it completely. He wishes that his consulting services would just "sell themselves." He is very good at what he does, and when a prospect becomes a client, they want to continue working with him.

What he doesn't like is how he *feels* about the selling part. He has a certain resistance toward it. He has to work himself up to go into a "sales call," and he gets all sweaty and anxious when it's time to deliver the proposal. He is uncomfortable throughout the sales meeting, knowing that questions about pricing and other objections will come up. When his latest prospect point-blank asked him if he knows how much less his competitors down the road are charging (yes, he's aware, those guys don't deliver half the value he does, thank you very much!), he felt guilty, ashamed even, and did not know what to say in return. Going through these sales calls is agonizing when he is constantly trying to justify his rates and prove himself, and—the worst part—Josh can't stand feeling needy. As irony would have it, this justifying approach neither wins him high-paying clients nor creates a good vibe around his business. Everybody loses.

Deep down, Josh wants to believe that there is a way to feel good about his business, his rates, and even selling, but he has no idea what's missing. The depth of his struggle around selling is making it hard to see the big-picture goal: the ability to scale up his business to enable his dream. Josh believed the formula for success was in the combination of his technical skills and his newly gained leadership and communication strategies from MBA school. Now he's not so sure.

And that is a *great* formula, except that it's not complete; it's a partial formula to business success. What is missing from this formula for creating true success and sustainability in your business is the necessary mindset shift around selling.

The complete formula is:

1. **Your Specialization / Expertise / Unique Skills & Talents**

   +

2. **Your Leadership / Communication / Business Acumen / "People Skills"**

   +

3. **(often the missing piece) Your Abundant Sales Mindset**

If you follow Josh's formula, which is essentially points one and two in the formula, you will absolutely create some marginal business success for yourself. So, if you want to create a business that just pays your bills and brings in some disposable income on top, you can accomplish that—points one and two will likely get you there.

But what if you want more? A lot more?

In the early months of my business, I was happy to have *any* sales at all, so the struggle that went into each transaction did not matter. After all, look at me, I was in business, and secretly, I was even a little proud of the struggle. Everybody knows that being in business is supposed to be hard, that selling is supposed to be a beast, but we accept it as the necessary evil to running a successful company. This was the story I was feeding myself until I stumbled across the brilliant work of Byron Katie, conveniently called *The Work*.

Katie invites you to inquire into your beliefs, which we will also do at length in this book. She believes that we weave a story—or a narrative, two terms used interchangeably throughout the book—around our beliefs so that we can easily justify those beliefs to ourselves. She asks you to challenge narrative. So, think of any situation or event where you formulated your own narrative. Now, answer Katie's two powerful questions about this narrative:

Is it true?
Can I absolutely know that it's true?

You may say yes to the first question and decide yes, it is true for you, but what about the second question? Can you absolutely, completely and objectively, know your narrative to be true? Earlier, we mentioned bringing your thinking under inquiry so that you can begin to see other useful and helpful narratives. Then you can choose to believe one that is helpful and useful for you.

For instance, say you had a prospect politely reject your proposal but not share their reasons. That is the event, the situation, so to speak. How you translate what happened is your narrative, and there are countless ways that could go. You might say that they found a "better deal" and went with your competitor. You may argue that the timing was bad for them and they'll come back down the road. Both are subjective narratives, and we cannot know either one to be 100% true, so can you choose the narrative that serves and supports you toward your goals? Can you be intentional about a useful and helpful narrative versus a hurtful and negative one? By the way, we will explore the prospect's reasons for not moving forward with us in greater detail later in the upcoming mindset shift chapters.

Using Byron Katie's powerful method, I was able to go from extreme dislike to a big love for selling, from a constant struggle to effortless authentic selling. I looked this "necessary evil" in the eye and turned it into the most fun and exciting part of my business. And I did it while charging premium rates and still delighting my customers and clients.

You, too, can have *all this* when you adopt an Abundant Sales Mindset—the question is whether you want this outcome *enough* to change your story about selling. The question is whether you want these results enough to be willing to inquire into your deep-rooted beliefs with vulnerability and honesty.

All my clients, peers, and contributors to this body of work and I said yes to that question, and if you did, too, it's time to look at exactly what we mean by an Abundant Sales Mindset.

MINDSETS AND LIMITING BELIEFS

WHAT IS A MINDSET?

A MINDSET IS A set Mind. Set on what? On a collection of ideas, stories, and thoughts that you hold to be true. If you have a mindset about a subject or a concept, these ideas and stories strongly resonate with you. The overall veracity of these ideas and stories is irrelevant; they are true for YOU; they make up your beliefs on the said subject. You have picked these up through your various life experiences and exposures to that subject matter. Now you have formed them into a belief system which your mind presents to you whenever that subject shows up in your life. This belief system dictates your feelings on the subject and is a heavy influence on all your related actions.

Unless you've spent years fine-tuning your awareness level, you do all this subconsciously. You are unaware of your own belief system without a conscious effort to think about it. It is even hard to discern between your belief system and who you are as a person. If your beliefs are particularly strong, you'll defend them by calling them out as needed, even if you are unaware of doing so. For example: "I told you I'm not good at sales. It's just not who I am. It's not my personality. It's not in my genes. It's not for me."

As far as you're concerned, that's just the way things are. The earth is round, the day is twenty-four hours long, and sales is hard for you. Those are all equal facts from your lens of the world, and no amount of positive thinking can change your mind. While the first two are indeed facts, the last one is a story you choose to believe. There is no such thing as "That's just the way I am!" because all humans are capable of change. The more accurate phrase would be, "That's just the way I choose to be!"

Mindsets can be insanely powerful. The problem arises when you have not *decided* on your mindset with intention and clarity, but rather, let it form haphazardly throughout your life experiences and interactions with people. In this case, your mindset took shape throughout your upbringing, education, and work, and it grew stronger as you fed it with validation of these beliefs. We see what we want to see in this world. If you already know what you want to see, you shall find evidence of it, especially here in the Internet age.

Say you have gone about your world with a firmly held belief that selling is hard. You will have easily found thousands of examples that seem to prove this is indeed the case. As a result, your belief got stronger, your defenses bigger, and your arguments more powerful, and now you fight to keep this belief firmly in its place. Never mind that this belief is not at all serving you; it's your religion and you're keeping it. This is called confirmation bias: the tendency to search for, interpret, favor, and recall information in a way that confirms one's preexisting beliefs or hypotheses. What is wrong with that? You are entitled to your opinions and viewpoints, after all; it's a free world.

Nothing is wrong with it *at all* unless something is amiss in the world you desire to create for yourself. If the firmly held belief that "sales is hard" is serving you well in your business, then all is well. If this belief is enabling you to reach your highest aspirations and fulfill your biggest ambitions, then carry on. If your perspective on selling is not in any conflict with how you desire to run your enterprise, and if, at the end of every conversation with a prospect, you feel true to yourself and aligned to your values, then your belief *is* working for you and your mindset is serving you just fine.

But if you have started to question this approach to growing your business in the long term, and if there is a nagging sense at the back of your mind that something doesn't feel right and there could be a better way, it may be time to bring your beliefs under inquiry and to examine your mindset.

Good News: Your Mindset is Not Fixed

Some things in life are fixed: Your DNA and your blood type, for example. Your mindset isn't one of those things. Your mindset has never been fixed. You can decide from this moment that you will develop and nurture and create a different mindset. You can adopt new beliefs that enable you, rather than block you. You can set the foundation of an intentional mindset that actually moves you toward your dream future, instead of fooling you into believing that such a future does not exist for you. But it won't exist if you listen to that voice, and it most certainly won't create itself by magic. You need to do the work today to enable that future tomorrow and it comes down to choosing between either an Abundance Mindset or a Scarcity Mindset. Let's define those now.

ABUNDANCE VS. SCARCITY

We all came into the world with a perfectly open and receptive mind. For some of us, our mindset took the shape of an Abundance Mindset, and for others, it took the shape of a Scarcity Mindset. These mindsets lean either toward abundance or scarcity and that starts with your definition of success.

We all crave success. Now, if you lean toward more of a scarcity mindset, you see success as being limited in quantity, as it were. You see the success of others as a limiting factor to your own; success to you is a zero-sum game, much like cutting a cake: if your competitor or peer got a bigger piece, you are naturally left with a smaller piece. Or, worse yet, since there are only so many pieces to go around, you may fear you would be left without any cake altogether, like poor Milton in the movie *Office Space*.

A scarcity mindset sets you up for failure through self-sabotage; it severely limits your potential. Plus, it is annoying and frustrating. A scarcity mindset robs you of joy, the ultimate reward for the labors of an entrepreneur. A scarcity mindset is selfish and jealous, and it wants you to fail. But if you lean toward more of an Abundance Mindset, you don't see success as a zero-sum game at all. You believe in the inherent quality of abundance, a way of being and showing up in your business and your life that says you are enough, and you can have anything you want. Success to you is nothing like cake-cutting at an office party. Success to you is boundless, limitless, and of infinite measure; success grows and expands as you grow and expand your mind; success begets more success. The success of others inspires you because you can see that it is possible for them, and that reinforces the fact that it is *entirely* possible for you, too.

The Abundance Mindset helps you find your power. It helps you stand on your own two feet and say no to the need for validation, permission, acceptance and praise from others. It helps you exercise indifference toward the fears of being judged and criticized. The abundance mindset allows you to be ALL you can be, without excuses, without limitations, without that constant voice of criticism and doubt in your head. The Abundance Mindset is your highest self at work, serving your best interests and inspiring you to be a vessel to serve others. It leads you to a meaningful life and a thriving business.

Let's look at a sales example. With a Scarcity Mindset, you would try to fit any sales prospect into the mold of what you have to offer, rather than being of true service to what they need. By being of true service, a phrase we will use throughout the book, we mean that you have your prospect's best interest at heart, you show up with a genuine desire to serve them, and together, you set out to discover what would best fulfill that interest. You know you are being of true service when you can turn away a prospect who may be better off without your product or service. An Abundance Mindset always leads you to true service. If what your prospect truly needs is someone else's service or product, your scarcity mindset would want to convince them otherwise, whereas with an Abundance Mindset, you know that the business opportunity was not rightfully yours to begin with. Given this perspective, you would see that your job at that point is to act as a connector to help this prospect go from where they are to their next stepping-stone, and you would do this gladly because opportunities are abundant and better ones shall come your way. A scarcity mindset comes from a place of lack and rejection. If scarcity thoughts arise as you get into conversation with your prospects, such as "I've gotta get them to sign with me!" or "I need clients, and this may be the only one willing to pay my rates!," just know that the roots of such thoughts can be traced back to feelings of lack and rejection.

How, then, do you disempower these unfounded emotions that fabricate the worst possible outcome of every situation in your mind? By exposing your imagination to the polar opposite, such as: "There are hundreds of qualified candidates wanting to hire me. I am in high demand and really good at what I do." Since you cannot prove either story, why not believe the useful and helpful one instead? When you make this switch regularly, you will start to tap into the energy of abundance, because the truth is that you simply *cannot know* for a fact that there are *not* a thousand highly qualified people out there willing to work with you. So, if anything can be true, focus on the belief that empowers you, rather than the one that debilitates you. Doing this is essential for coming from a place of service because it helps you create the most attractive and inviting environment for the prospect.

As it turns out, you increase your chances of closing every deal if you come from a place of true abundance and are totally detached from the final outcome. An Abundance Mindset is inspiring and empowering *and* it works as we will set out to prove in this book.

GUIDING PRINCIPLE: YOUR MINDSET MUST ENABLE YOUR PATH AT ALL STAGES OF LIFE, NOT BLOCK IT

YOUR MINDSET HAS TO work *for* you, not *against* you. Many people live their whole lives with mindsets that work against them, not for them, and of which they are often unaware. Think of the finger-pointing grumpy neighbor who blames the outside world for all his miseries. Or the victim-playing friend who expects you to feel sorry for her all the time. Or the aspiring writer who has every excuse not to write the book he says he wants to write. These are prime examples of individuals who have a mindset that blocks their own paths. They are unaware or dishonest with themselves, and thus continue to live in the bubble of scarcity mindset. Instead, imagine if they were operating from a total honesty filter—where they were being honest with themselves and open to see their experience from an abundance mindset that enables—rather than blocks—them.

Releasing the Scarcity Mindset, 5% at a Time

But most of us want overnight makeovers. We want to jump from not confident at all to 100% confident, or from hating sales to loving sales, without doing the work or walking through the stages in between. But what if you could walk these middle steps from where you are in a way that feels accessible and even pleasant? Enter: the 5% solution, which one of my role models, Jason Goldberg, author of *Prison Break* (an excellent book!) and creator of *The Playful Prosperity Program* (an amazing program from my first-hand experience) developed as a useful tool to help make big leaps accessible to us.

The 5% solution is a brilliant alternative that teaches you to be patient with yourself as you slowly shift away from your scarcity mindset. And it takes time to shift a lifetime's way of thinking to a better one, no matter how sold (no pun intended!) you are on the target belief. With this tool, you can begin to celebrate your teeny-tiny incremental progress as you implement powerful mindset shifts in your daily decisions and actions.

I talked about all this with Jason because his story is another great example of transformative mindset shifts. In his coaching and speaking business, Jason does not see himself as someone who sells at all. He sees every interaction as an exploration with another human being to see if it makes sense to offer them access to one of his gifts, with a mindset that he is first and foremost in the relationship business. He described the energy of abundance this way: "It will put you fully in a detached, committed, loving, focused, sincere place to explore with this person." Which is precisely where you need to be to serve the person in front of you.

Jason introduced the 5% solution by putting it in the context of what he calls in his book a Prison Break Question (PBQ). This type of question has a basic format: "If I knew . . . what would I do?"

The PBQ question Jason asked himself when he was struggling was this: "If I were 5% more professional, as a coach or a speaker or a human being, how would I show up?" This frame-up would help him take small steps toward a large vision.

Some other questions that you can try using the two tools Jason shared are:

How would I show up if . . .

- I were 5% more confident on the next prospecting call?
- I listened 5% more actively?
- I slowed down 5% more than the last time when I rushed the prospect?
- I probed 5% more about their objections?
- I believed 5% deeper in my value as a professional?
- I enjoyed my sales conversations 5% more than yesterday?

The 5% is an arbitrary number; the idea is a small amount of improvement on a consistent basis. All of us can do a tiny bit better today than yesterday and repeat this again day after day until, one day, we look back and we've come so far that we hardly recognize the old version of ourselves.

Now that you have a basic understanding of scarcity versus abundance mindset, you are ready to apply the mindset work and see if it works for you. Let's go there now.

DOING THE MINDSET WORK

YOU'RE HERE. YOU'VE MADE it this far. You are convinced that your mindset must enable your path, and not block it. Great! Now let's talk strategy.

Exactly how do we do this mindset work? It's not like taking the stairs or washing the dishes, where you have a clear idea as to what needs to be done, even if you have zero enthusiasm for the task. Mindset work is not something you can see or touch or hear. It is a silent shift in your thoughts and beliefs that happens internally.

How, then, do we make it more tangible?

First, begin by observing yourself. Stand back and observe your behavior in the context of sales and selling in your business. In meditation circles, there is a beautiful term used to describe this mode of self-reflection: the Seat of Awareness.

Imagine watching yourself from your seat of awareness; let's say there is a new prospect interested in your services. You likely have a process for reaching back out to the prospect. Here are a few questions to ask yourself:

- How do I think about this prospect?
- What am I saying to myself about him/her?
- How does it feel in my body to have this conversation?
- What am I really thinking about?
- How am I judging myself or the prospect?
- What is my real priority here?

Slow down as you probe into your thinking with these questions, and see if you can come at the situation from the view of an impartial outside observer. What you are looking for here in your thinking is called a "limiting belief."

WHAT ARE LIMITING BELIEFS AND GUIDING PRINCIPLES?

A LIMITING BELIEF IS a belief that limits your possibilities. A limiting belief can be a gem, though—shine a light upon it and you will see, perhaps for the first time, the true limitation in your way: your own beliefs. No outside circumstance can hold you back as much as your own limiting beliefs.

Example One: You are capable of creating ten times your current revenue, but your limiting beliefs about money, worthiness, and circumstances have kept you boxed in.

Example Two: You want joy in your business, but your limiting belief that building a successful business is full of hardship and struggle makes it impossible for you to find this joy.

A Guiding Principle is a tool that helps you to address your Limiting Beliefs and, as you do so, to recognize your ability to move beyond these beliefs and step into your power. When you see that your Limiting Beliefs are between you and your goals, you are ready to dismantle them, and Guiding Principles show you how to do just that.

Here is how these two integrate. As you pause to question your beliefs, you'll take your first step toward identifying the limiting ones. As you do this, you will start to realize some or most of your beliefs are in fact sabotaging your goals and dreams. But don't be discouraged by this; every successful entrepreneur has gone through not one but several stages of uncovering and dismantling limiting beliefs, and continues to do so. In fact, to lighten things up, I like to think of my limiting beliefs as a misinterpretation or misunderstanding that happened a while ago, and can be fixed up with a new perspective.

To create your new Abundance Mindset around selling, first we help you to map out all your associated limiting beliefs and then we have you bring them into inquiry by asking the right questions to help you see whether (A) a belief is indeed false and not serving you and (B) if so, then we share a few guiding principles to help you to dismantle your limiting beliefs, which, once uncovered and put to inquiry, lose their power over you!

So it's simply a matter of self-correction, of finding your limiting beliefs and following the right Guiding Principles that counter those beliefs and allowing the new mindset to slowly emerge.

Hit Pause on Your Personal Preferences

Imagine this: What if your personal preferences were not the compass for a day or a week? What would you observe in your world if you could temporarily set your personal preferences aside?

Let's define personal preferences first. Do you hear yourself saying any of this?

- "I love this part of my business."
- "I hate that part of my work."
- "I like this prospect."
- "I don't like that client."
- "I like this vendor."
- "I don't like talking to people."
- And on and on and on, as your inner voice makes snap judgments a hundred times an hour!

What if you could set aside these personal preferences—your likes and dislikes—long enough to see the situation before you in a different light?

In his masterpiece, *The Surrender Experiment*, Michael A. Singer talks about the incredible opportunities that he was able to *see* once he set aside all those snap judgments. As he trained himself to quiet the like/dislike voice in his head and to be more present with the situation in front of him, he saw everything more clearly.

What was his new internal compass, then, if he was not using the like/dislike to guide him? His observations of the present moment! He would ask himself questions such as "What is this situation really showing me?" or "What could happen if I took this opportunity?" He learned to quiet his internal judge and to be curious and open.

When I first read this passage in *The Surrender Experiment*, I realized how heavily the like/dislike voice guides my own decisions. Or how that voice blinds me to the full picture as I make snap decisions silently. I did not know this about myself until that moment, and then it was so clear in hindsight. Since then, I've made it a point to quiet that voice at least long enough to absorb the situation from an impartial viewpoint.

What about you? How many times might you have dismissed an opportunity simply based on a notion of your likes and dislikes? Do you even know why you like/dislike something or someone? The ultimate challenge here is to stay open and present after your mind makes its milliseconds-long assessment through the like/dislike lens, to be open to other possibilities in the story and to stay present here and now rather than going off with our anxiety into the future or our worries into the past.

Example: You meet a new person at a networking event. They immediately remind you of someone you didn't get on with back at your old job. You subconsciously put your guard up; in other words, you close up. You've made the snap judgment that you don't and won't like them anyway, even if you continue to chat away politely. Unbeknownst to you, they pick up on your vibe and they too close up. The possibility of a great relationship is already tainted before it even begins.

But what if you could disregard your past experience—after all, everyone deserves a second chance—and stay open and present in this situation? Where might this opportunity lead you without your snap judgments?

The funny thing is that we often don't even know the true reason behind our likes and dislikes, but when we get curious, we create room for reconsideration, and sometimes we change our minds. For instance, how many times have you changed your mind about something that you thought for sure you didn't like but then, somehow, you started to like it after a new experience? Or vice-versa? This applies to food, people, activities, movies, books, and so on—even to sales.

We are trained to judge, and we do it in a blink of an eye, but it's just a habit and, like all habits, it can be reversed. As you learn to think differently about sales in the next chapters, you will retrain and recondition your mind to be curious, to slow down, to stay open, and to see the full picture from an objective view. You may be surprised by how much more you will see, often for the first time.

THE FIVE MINDSETS

THE FIVE MINDSETS THAT we'll cover next create the foundation of a new paradigm around sales and selling. I've chosen these specific five because they come up again and again in the early stages of transforming one's old thinking about sales, and they build the momentum needed to help you approach it all from a new fresh perspective. By mastering these five mindsets, serving will go from an idea in your head to a natural way of being and showing up in your business, and everything else will begin to fall into place.

Here are the five mindsets:

Mindset One: You are not selling. You are serving.
Mindset Two: Enable your new identity to emerge.
Mindset Three: Care about your prospects and show it.
Mindset Four: Charge appropriately for your services.
Mindset Five: Address voiced and unvoiced objections.

MINDSET ONE: YOU ARE NOT SELLING. YOU ARE SERVING.

NOBODY WANTS TO BE sold to. Not you. Not me. Not the most eager buyer in the world. We want to come to that decision of our own volition. We want to buy. We want to decide when to buy. We want to love what we buy. And we want to feel great about buying.

How do you help us get there? You serve.

And here's the golden rule of serving: You never *ever* want to be selling. Selling needs to happen as the natural, organic outcome of what you do.

What do you do, then? You serve. You serve in the most genuine, passionate, and intense way you know how. You serve and serve and keep serving.

What does it even mean to serve? It means to come from a place of total service—your goal in every interaction, every conversation, every promotion, every marketing campaign, and every website offer changes from selling to serving the person in front of you. Your internal dialogue changes from "I'm selling" to "I'm serving." You won't need a *selling* strategy anymore, because you'll have a *serving* strategy. You won't have sales calls; you'll have serving calls.

This simple and subtle shift will set you free. Free of the need to close, the need to "get a client," the need to sell or get a signed contract. Those outcomes will be easily fulfilled when you shift your focus to simply serving the person in front of you.

Serving is not automatic; it needs to be learned and practiced. Yet serving is also natural, rewarding, and, most of all, it feels good. As I've shared before, this "detail" of feeling good is important because it's a clear sign that you are serving. If you've been trained to sell rather than to serve, changing will require a beginner's mind and a willingness to retrain on your part. Your sales tactics and strategies may yet have an application, but if they were working for you as well as you had hoped they might, you would not be here right now.

Serving sets you free so you can set aside your tactics and strategies, drop your agenda, go into the next "sales meeting," and just be there to serve.

Serving Changed Everything for Me

Everything changed for me when I truly started to come from a place of service and give up the other goals such as closing a client, "getting" a new client, or selling to a client. The pressure to close had evaporated, and I had always hated—let me be clear, HATED—that pressure, because if I were the prospective client, which I have been many times while looking to hire my own coaches, I could always smell the desire to close from a mile away. And I would run from it, every single time.

By the same token, I could also feel the generosity of those who never pressured me, who totally served me and created an incredible experience in that interaction, whether it were for fifteen minutes or two hours. This sense of generosity through serving was so profound that I felt naturally drawn to working with those people.

No, We Are Not Giving Away the Farm!

A point of clarification: serving does not mean we give of our time and energy for free in hopes that the customer wants to work with us. It's easy to confuse the two. You are still very much in business, and the whole point here is to help you *raise* the bar on everything, including your business revenue, not to take away business while having you run in circles for free.

This is where the counterintuitive part comes in, and I warn you, it's the first of many in the mindset world. You may think that getting the client to close on the deal or getting the customer to hit the buy button is the fastest way to generate income. Yes, closing and buying need to happen, but rushing to get there actually pushes them away, and makes it harder over time to build the type of business that you love.

On the other hand, serving may seem to be the "slow path" to get there, yet it's precisely the slowing down that creates space—space to build trust with your prospect, space to show that you really care, space to go deep and understand their real needs. As we said earlier, it's a nice little paradox of life that when we slow down, we, in fact, get ahead and win.

The trust that you create by slowing down allows you to get to the goals behind the goals with your prospect. This the distinction between their outer goal and their inner goal, the *real* reason they are seeking your help. Example: Your prospect's outer goal may be securing an IT service provider to set up their new phone lines and computer systems, but their inner goal is to feel safe, protected from hackers, and to have someone they can trust when things go wrong. Slowing down will help you understand these inner goals through a deeper conversation and thus more easily earn the prospect's business. Slowing down builds deep trust in your market in the long term, which is the true path to sustainability in your business.

GUIDING PRINCIPLE: SERVING IS YOUR COMPETITIVE ADVANTAGE

SERVING GIVES YOU THE ultimate competitive advantage. Even in this new economy where we are more aware, better educated, and more socially conscious, very few business owners *truly believe and operate* in this model, and this is precisely what customers and clients wish more businesses would do. Many may operate under the pretext of serving, but that can only take them so far. You should seize this competitive advantage.

But our nemesis, the rush to close, is stubborn and impatient. It blinds our vision. It skews our values. It makes us uncomfortable and uneasy, and that's only our end of it as "sellers." What is happening in your customer's mind, unbeknownst to you, is far worse.

The pressure to close gives off a sense of desperation and neediness on our part, one that Steve Chandler, the godfather of coaching (as per his unofficial title), calls creepy. My favorite saying by him is this: "Needy is creepy. No wonder stalking is a crime." So why risk coming across as needy, or—worse—creepy, when we can come across as professionals in the act of serving?

All you have to do to test this concept, or any others in this book for that matter, is to turn it around on its head: You be the prospect now. How would *you* respond if a business owner came to you from a place of true service rather than following an agenda? How would you respond to a true professional in the act of serving you, versus an amateur who clearly needs your business more than you need their service? How would you open up with your real challenges and frustrations, and your hopes for a solution, and your real purpose in all of this? How relaxed and calm would you be in your experience with this business when you know for a fact that they have your best interests at heart, even above their own, driven by a philosophy that either you win together or you part ways?

Would this business not have a competitive advantage over others in your mind as a potential customer? Even if you are not ready to buy now, would you not naturally think of this business when you are ready to buy in the future? This is in no small part because of how they made you feel: comfortable, safe, valued, important, and worth their time and energy without any strings attached.

The deposits we create through serving pay dividends and accumulate over time. Selling is self-serving. Serving is all-serving.

Adopting a new mindset starts the breakdown of the limiting beliefs that resist it. So every mindset will set out to crack and then ultimately disempower the limiting beliefs which resist it. For Mindset One, "You are not selling, you are serving," we will explore the two primary limiting beliefs and then disempower them gently but firmly.

LIMITING BELIEF ONE: "SALES IS SLEAZY. I DON'T WANT TO BE SLEAZY."

Our culture, along with the help of the media and entertainment world, has conditioned our brains to flash those unsavory images when we hear words like sales or selling, and for most of us, we can also throw in the upbringing factor. A possible exception may be if you were the son or daughter of a successful businessman or woman who passed on the importance and virtues of honest selling. Even then, I've met such people who grew up with a positive affinity toward selling, only to let the strong cultural conditioning turn them against sales in their adult years.

The bottom line is that we often see sales as sleazy and we are very distrustful of it. This is a limiting belief, not a fact, and as we begin to integrate the mindset of serving, not selling, we will prove it.

Just as sales can be sleazy, immoral, unsavory, disreputable, and shady, it can also be honest, authentic, fun, joyful, and effortless. You can embody this way of selling when you come from a place of service, when your intention shifts from selling to being of total service.

How? Because you are no longer driven by a hidden agenda. You are not trying to be someone you're not. You are not self-serving, and therefore you have nothing to hide. When these false pretenses fall away, when you set aside your latest-and-greatest sales tactics to trick a customer or client, you are left with your honest self, with a product or service that you completely believe in, and with your innate desire to be of service. In short, it is impossible for sales to feel sleazy when you are serving.

"I Am Morally Finding It Hard to Be That Sleazy Person!"

This mindset was a particular challenge for one of my clients, Anita Weber. Anita is a Principal Solutions Consultant based out of the Gold Coast of Australia, and she is remarkably good at her craft. She is methodical, thorough, and delivers above and beyond on her services every single time. She looks out for her clients and holds herself to the highest degree of quality and service. Anita also hates selling because, as she said, "That's not who I am."

Anita is an introvert; she speaks in a quiet, low voice; she is more of a listener and observer. This used to be her take on sales:

"I find that technical people are very introverted and we tend to like to be isolated and just get our work done. We can be team players and work in agile environments, because we like structure. However, the sales and client management area is outside our comfort zone as it has many dynamics that are constantly changing per client and per conversation—which makes someone like myself feel awkward immediately."

She adds later on, "I also find sales is the most opposite skillset to a technical person. We like facts and explaining. Sales involves, dare I say, smooth talking and manipulating emotions."

In Anita's mind, a salesperson was an overzealous, highly sociable, enthusiastic guy or gal who never shut up and was constantly in your face. She wanted none of that, and I don't blame her; I don't either.

But is it true that you must be loud, overzealous, highly sociable, and enthusiastic in order to be a great salesperson? Is it true that you have to blab constantly and be in people's faces and have that "charming" aura about you in order to sell?

No, it is NOT true.

You *can* be effective at selling and stay true to exactly who you are, what values you stand for, and how you show up. It is not your personality that needs to change. It is your mindset that needs to shift in order to embrace a way of selling that integrates fully into who you want to be.

Anita was able to see this limitation in her beliefs and accomplish a breakthrough in our work. She held steadfast to the non-negotiable promise of being herself as she committed to bringing in the type of clients and revenue that would help her achieve her business goals and dreams. She was able to develop a mindset that supported this way of showing up, combined with authentic positioning, building deep trust, cultivating relationships and learning the art of having an authentic serving—not selling—conversation.

As Anita has found out through our work and her own growth and development, she can achieve her sales goals by staying true to who she is. She's learned to sell through trust and reputation, by building relationships, by focusing on the company's long-term benefits and positioning herself powerfully by serving. She did not have to compromise on her values after all, yet she decided to work more on her self-confidence and be more engaging by asking the right questions of the client, thus demonstrating her care in more vocal ways than before. And she does all this while still being herself.

These may not be the most natural tendencies for Anita, but they are not steering her away from her personality either. Rather, they are helping her enrich her identity into a much better version of herself while staying true to the high-integrity professional that she is.

Interrupt the Story and Rewrite the Script

Now that we have established why this limiting belief harms your business, let's get practical. How do you eradicate it and adopt the winning mindset of serving?

You do this by changing the narrative, which, as we said before, is entirely within your control, because your mindset is fluid, not fixed. Your current years- or decades-long narrative insists that sales is sleazy and even hard. You have heard it a thousand times without questioning it or interrupting it, much less replacing it with a new story. Good news: You wrote the script and you can rewrite it.

Next time you notice yourself even feel a slight cringe at the thought of sales, pause everything you are doing. The physical interruption is important to get your attention here. If you are driving, pull to the side of the road. If you are eating, put your utensils down. If you are talking to someone or in a meeting, excuse yourself. You get the idea.

Then immediately ask yourself: "What do I *choose to believe* in this moment?" As you ask this question, contemplate the words. Your old story may still be playing in the background, but you are now using the power of choice to interrupt and question that story. You can decide that you will no longer take this story at face value. You always have a choice where your beliefs are concerned, and the first step in unhinging yourself from the clasp of a limiting belief is by exercising your power to choose.

I've done this with my clients, and often, they are so struck by the question alone that the intended effect is achieved right away. We don't even have to answer the question to start disentangling ourselves from the limiting belief. We simply know that we now refuse to believe the old story.

As your old story comes under question, you open a door to new possibilities by rewriting the script. In the moment that you choose to believe a different story, you create a small internal shift. This subtle internal shift, which may be barely perceptible at first, is beyond powerful, because you are now seeing your world through a different lens, which will in turn lead to new decisions and actions on your part. The previous lens screamed "sales is sleazy" or "sales is hard." This new one declares "I am serving; I am not selling."

Your limiting belief is now out of luck. Your old script is deleted. Your old story has lost all support from its master, you, so it's about to obliterate itself. And you are now entering into your new mindset. You are choosing to write your own story. You're awesome.

Ok, Wait, There's a Little More

So, everything still goes, but that's not the whole story. You see, your beliefs needed a lifetime to take form, so they are rock solid; they want to endure. We just took a hammer to them and banged them up a bit. We cracked the surface. It is a great start, but it is a work that needs to continue to make the shift permanent. We still need to disempower them, remember?

The weight of your limiting belief is directly proportional to the amount of work you need to put in to undo its effect. What does this mean? If you adopted this belief somewhere at the workplace, say, in the last couple of years, your odds of eradicating the belief quickly are higher than if you have lived with this belief for a decade or longer.

You have created a new awareness, and the only way to keep it up is to practice. Practice the interruption technique; practice asking the question "What do I *choose to believe* in this moment?" over and over; practice answering it with the new belief that you want to integrate and the new script that you want to write; practice repeating the whole thing over and over again. Practice until you automatically stop yourself, answer the question before you hear it, and carry on as if nothing has happened. Over time, your new mindset will become your default, and over time, you will truly see sales as service. You will feel it, you will speak it, you will embody it, and you will know it to be true.

Until then, practice. Pros practice; amateurs expect miracles right away. You are a pro, right? So practice.

LIMITING BELIEF TWO: "SALES IS SO HARD. SALES IS SUCH A STRUGGLE."

Have you ever heard yourself or a fellow business partner describe sales as hard? Have you thought it, even if you haven't said it out loud? Have you felt a hardship and struggle around selling?

In my coaching with new business owners and entrepreneurs, I can see that the excitement around their product or service is palpable. They are bright individuals who know they can make a difference in the world by sharing their brilliant ideas. They are convinced that their work is meant for the betterment of the world. They are excited and hard at work figuring out the nuances of bringing this product or service to market. Then

I ask them about their real challenge and, invariably, it comes down to selling.

The stories go something like this:

- "I'm not really a sales person, so sales is hard for me."
- "I'm more of an introvert so sales doesn't come naturally to me."
- "I hear sales is the hardest part of being in business and I totally agree."
- "I am avoiding the selling like the plague. I can see myself struggling with it."
- "I feel conflicted about selling my services or charging much for them; it just feels so hard."

Here's one thing you can be certain of: Whatever you perceive sales to be, it will become precisely that. If you think sales is hard, it will be insurmountably so. If you think selling is a struggle, it will be the struggle of your life.

This is the manifestation of your limiting belief. What you believe, you manifest in your world.

Your thoughts may sound harmless, but they aren't. Your beliefs may seem irrelevant to reality, but they couldn't be more related. Just because we cannot see them or touch them does not mean they don't influence us. Think about it: You can't see electricity or heat or cold or love or hate, but they all have massive influence in how we live and work and play, and you wouldn't argue for a second that they don't exist every bit as much as you and I do.

Sales is Not Easy or Hard. It's Neutral.

Eckhart Tolle, a phenomenal spiritual master, makes a distinction in life between what he calls "form" and "formless." He suggests that much of the pain we experience in our lives comes from our attachment to form and our lack of awareness of the formless dimension of life. In truth, the things that heavily influence our behavior, decisions and actions are often formless. Our limiting beliefs, for example, are formless, and so it's been easy to neglect them while chasing the form dimension of life. But now is the time to pay acute attention to the formless, for it is the underlying problem to your selling woes.

The first step to breaking down this limiting belief is to think of sales as neutral. Sales is neither good nor bad, neither easy nor difficult; it is a process that enables you to bring your business to life.

You can keep it at this neutral level and attach no essence to it if you choose. By doing only this much, you'll have already questioned the limiting belief that dictates sales is hard. You'll have cracked at the edges of this limiting belief. You'll have lessened its influence over you.

Now let's see if there is any truth to your limiting belief. Is sales really hard? What if it's hard some of the time and easy other times? Would that not make it more neutral then? What if you sold naturally and organically to some of your customers, but experienced extreme difficulty with others? Would it not be fair to "grade" sales on an objective scale than just by the sum of your bad experiences? Would that make sales hard, easy, somewhat hard, or somewhat easy? It's hard to say (no pun intended) but what we do know is this: Your limiting belief is not entirely true, is it?

To help you think of sales as neutral in another way, consider this: What if you did not refer to it as selling? After all, we are shifting your focus from closing the prospect or getting the deal to being of true service. We are asking you to concentrate on how to be all about the customer, rather than about yourself.

This is the thinking that creates the new experience for you, so what if this experience were not even called selling? Selling is an outcome, a natural occurrence after the fact. We do not have to "do" any selling, so we can stop calling it by that term. We are moving away from selling and creating the experience of serving.

GUIDING PRINCIPLE: YOU'RE NOT SELLING ANYWAY

So, IT DOES NOT matter if sales is easy or hard—that is no longer relevant. It's completely gone from the equation, because you're not selling. What a relief. Let's focus on serving instead. Is serving hard? Would you describe being of service to a prospect as a struggle, as a challenge, as a thing you would want to avoid?

Whenever I've asked this question of any business owner, the answer has invariably been no. They love being of service. They feel comfortable. It feels right. It feels good to show up in front of a prospect or on the phone, and to be of total service. This way of being comes easily and naturally to them. Remember that feeling good is a major indicator that you are serving, and what's more, it's also a natural state of being and showing up for your business.

To make this more tangible, consider the last "sales call" you had with a prospect, and replay it from the start, except this time, see yourself coming from a place of total service. You are not on an agenda; you are there to serve. Serve, serve, and serve. See yourself asking questions that pertain to understanding their needs and fears, to help them see their problem more clearly, to gain their trust and to engage them in a meaningful conversation that can go in any direction that the prospect chooses.

My guess is that you are far more comfortable doing this, because even if you are not entirely sure how to operate in this mode, you know how *not* to operate. You know this difference because when you are on the receiving end of a sales call, your internal radar picks up on cues to selling. You know how to stop doing the things that get on your own nerves when you are being "sold to."

A wonderful benefit of serving—rather than selling—is that you can begin to relax. You can take a deep breath and slow down. You can get back in your body and become more present. You know there's nowhere to get to, no agenda to complete, no goal to achieve. This mindset teaches you to trust the process and allow the relationship between you and the prospect to form through mutual trust and understanding, through the time and attention that you are investing in them. As you do this, you will arouse the interest of this prospect. They will be curious as to how you want to solve the problem for them, and that's when you can start sharing how it would look if you worked together.

Let Them Lean Into You

A great visual for this comes from my amazing voice teacher, Sally Morgan, an incredibly talented coach who teaches Broadway stars about how best to use their voices, their instruments. Sally was coaching me on how to become a better speaker, especially when I was on panel interviews. One of her rules is this: You never ever want to lean into your audience, because if you do, they instantly lean back. They feel their personal space is being invaded. They may even get a little suspicious. They may even tune you out until they find their comfortable place again, if at all. The best way to get the attention of your audience and to captivate them, Sally continues, is to get them to *lean into you.* It is your job to draw them out with the right questions, the right words, the right tone and volume of voice, and the right intention behind every word.

How do we then get our prospect to lean into us? This naturally happens when you stop selling and start serving. When you are of service, you are showing real understanding and care through active listening. You are not assuming what your prospect wants, nor are you assuming that you have the solution. You are going into that phone call or meeting without any assumptions. Your only job is to be of service. Your only concern is to deliver this service to the prospect. If, when that prospect leaves the call or the meeting, they think to themselves that they feel you care, that you really are someone who gets what they need and why they need it, you have both won. The rewards may show up tomorrow or next year, but serving earns you units of trust and these units will add up to a flood down the road. Keep earning them.

Yes, You Can Serve Your Way to a Highly Profitable Business

When I share this first mindset, "You are not selling. You are serving." one of the more common reactions is skepticism. "Yes, that's nice," one business owner told me in our conversation, "but can you really 'serve' [with air quotes] your way to a highly profitable business?"

If you, too, are wondering whether this mindset is too naïve or not serious enough for real business success, real dollars, and real profit, you'd be sharing my peer's skepticism . . . and you'd be wrong.

My experience and that of my clients is a resounding yes—you *can* serve your way to a highly profitable business, because when you serve, you are showing yourself and your prospect the ultimate level of respect. You are saying, "I know my own value, I understand your problem and your needs, and I am confident I can help you. Let's see if we are the right fit to work together in a successful business relationship."

Being of service requires that you be true to yourself. Your first obligation in the business is to yourself. This is not selfish; this is a necessity if you want to bring your absolute best to clients and customers. How you price your services or products is key in integrating this mindset fully into your business.

Most of us think our first obligation is to our client. This assumption is the root cause of the mild resentment some business owners have for their clients. Self-sacrifice leads to this resentment. Don't be a hero here. Of course your clients are important, but not at the expense of your obligation first to YOU and your own needs.

The way you take care of yourself is by knowing your value and respecting your needs in business so you can show up at your best for others. This may sound "selfish" in the old-world model of thinking, but it is precisely why you can serve at your highest, because you've taken care of your own values and boundaries first. We will cover more about this paradox in Mindset Four.

Which Designer Would You Choose?

Recently, my husband and I decided to renovate our master bathroom. We were going to gut the entire room and design our dream zen bathroom, so we started to look for the most highly recommended designers and contractors. We interviewed exactly two, each on the opposite end of the spectrum, one on the end of selling, the other on the end of serving.

The first designer exchanged a few emails with us, and then suggested that she come by our house for a two-hour consultation to see whether she can take on the project and to give us an estimate. This consultation would cost us $375 upfront, but she was kind enough to credit it toward the project, should we hire her. Even as my intuition sent me warning signs about paying for this consultation, we decided to go ahead, to do our "due diligence" as my husband said. From the minute she came over, I knew in my mind that I was paying for this consultation, and I wanted to see a really good value.

And the two hours proceeded to be what I consider a total waste of our time and money. She was not a good match. She crushed my enthusiasm with her pessimistic approach to such projects, and recounted countless stories of how things had gone so wrong and she had come in and saved the day. Oh, and she would not give us an estimate of the entire project until we hired her, and this part flabbergasted me. We decided not to proceed with her.

In hindsight, I am almost certain that the upfront fee of the consultation was the part that really bothered me in this setup: charging before serving. This designer was not willing to invest a free minute in the relationship or to earn our trust as she prospected us for a high-dollar project. There was no up-front investment of time and energy on her part, nor any real show of care and compassion or zeal for getting the project.

The second designer and his project manager showed up at our house and spent two hours with us going over everything we needed for our dream bathroom; they came back with a twenty-five page, detailed, itemized, line-by-line estimate of what our project would cost if we should work with them. They invested another two hours to review and discuss. When we went back to them with a major change request to the project, which required a brand-new proposal, they gladly updated the proposal and sent us a new estimate. This does not even take into account all the research and prep time they spent on our project outside of direct interactions, prior to us paying them a dime or giving them an indication that we would indeed hire them.

Even when, at one point, my husband and I decided to back out of the whole thing, we knew that if we ever hired anyone to do this project, it would be them. We went off on a trip to think about it and when we talked about it again, we just knew. Two weeks later, we hired them for our $40k project.

It felt right, and it was right. They had put so much credit forth in building trust and assuring us that we would have our dream bathroom. Before hiring them, I checked half a dozen references on them, and their past clients raved about them openly. In situations when things had gone awry, as they often do with house renovation and construction-type projects, it was how each situation was handled that translated to volumes of praise. This company happened to be extremely successful and booked for business, yet they made the time and put forth the energy to treat us—a single client—as if we mattered the most.

So why did we hire the second designer over the first designer? In summary, it's because the one we hired was coming from a true place of service. In other words, they astonished us from start to finish.

When was the last time you astonished your clients? When was the last time you served your customers so well that they felt compelled to tell you or someone about it? That is the mindset of serving versus selling, and it translates across all types of businesses and industries.

How to Be of Service in the Coaching Profession

The coaching profession has exploded in the last two decades. We're not talking about sports coaches here, but, rather, coaches in business, career, personal growth and development, and life in general. The benefits of having a business or personal coach on your team or by your side have been proven again and again. So the desire to have a coach in business or at the workplace has never been stronger, and our culture has never advocated the idea of coaching more positively. This, then, should be a great time for all coaches.

The numbers tell a different story, though. The yearly income level of most coaches falls below the $50,000 mark, with the outliers in the six- or seven-figure range. What are these outlier coaches doing differently? Are they vastly better at their craft? Are they well-connected to a wealthy population who are willing to pay their fees? Are they just lucky? This has been my field of work since 2010, so it's also been a deep area of interest and curiosity.

My years of research and networking led me to this simple truth: Every coach in the six- or seven-figure range has a massive abundance mindset toward money, and those in the low five-figure range operate from a scarcity mindset. What's more, this is not about the quality of the coaching or the knowledge and expertise of the coach; some of the best coaches are hardly making ends meet. No, this all comes down to the mindset of the coach around money, self-worth, and value.

So how does this tie into the serving vs. selling mindset?

The coaches who are in the scarcity mindset are those who most aim to sell and who most hate selling, to boot. They came into this profession to help people, and this is the "hard part" of their business. They struggle with it. Their aversion to selling their services has played a major role in how they have priced themselves. Competition and insecurity drive their prices rather than value and ROI, and often the direction is downward. They are trying to please rather than serve their ideal clients. They are doing thirty-minute teaser sessions to figure out what the client needs and then quickly pitching them a package. They are worried about how the client will react to their prices, so they rush the sale or use scarcity tactics by pressuring the client. They fear rejection. They raise their prices by 5% at best every year, and feel guilty about it. They hate selling, they hate the struggle, they hate what they charge, and they get plenty of sympathy for it in online forums and groups. They are, in essence, a victim of their own mindset.

On the other hand, the rare coaches near the six- and seven-figure marks have an abundance mindset around selling and acquiring top-paying, happy, and easy clients. They approach selling from a place of true service. They spend quality time with their prospects. They invest upfront in the trust and the relationship and the care of every prospect. They know without a shadow of a doubt the value of their own work and the immense return on investment that follows. They've done this before, and they have a long list of testimonials that echoes this sentiment. They are pros at what they do, and they charge for it accordingly—it is not uncommon for this type of coach to charge more than the average coach's yearly income for a single client. Their clientele is not the rich and famous. Their clients are ordinary people with extraordinary dreams, and they want to work with a pro.

What the struggling coach does not understand is that they cannot attract this caliber of clientele when they don't have their own financial act together, when they are not living what they preach. This clientele is inspired by a prosperous coach who can take them to newer heights and help them create an abundance mindset by example, and that example is what the prosperous coach has already achieved in his or her own life. You must walk your talk, and choosing to serve will lead you there.

IS SERVING RIGHT FOR YOU?

If the serving—not selling—mindset has resonated with you on a deep level, if you wish you could do business this way and turn your selling struggles into a serving experience, all you have to do is decide that this is for you. You are the boss. You do not need to get permission from a higher authority or approval from a committee. You run the show, and you can start running it this way tomorrow.

But it's possible that serving will not speak to you right away. If so, I would urge you to ask yourself why. For instance, maybe your best friend had a business and he went into it with the idealistic view of being of service, and now he is out of business! Maybe you know "successful" business owners that have no interest in serving, and yet they make a ton of money. These examples are real, and even if you don't have full visibility into the whole situation, they can still skew your vision.

So adopting this mindset may bring up the familiar inner enemy of all paradigm shifts, Resistance (yes, with capital R). Steven Pressfield explains the role of inner Resistance brilliantly in his book *Do the Work*, a must-read for anyone doing the inner work on mindset. The entire book is so genius that it's quotable, but here's what I've chosen to share:

"The enemy is Resistance. The enemy is our chattering brain, which, if we give it so much as a nanosecond, will start producing excuses, alibis, transparent self-justifications, and a million reasons why we can't/shouldn't/won't do what we know we need to do."

So the question is what to do about it if indeed you want to come from a place of service in your business but you feel the resistance in the way. What's the next step?

Well, you forge ahead. You create momentum and experiment with the new ideas we covered in this chapter. You take a risk. You step outside your comfort zone and tell yourself to trust the process. You allow yourself to do the uncomfortable and to see how it plays out. You decide that you are worth the highest level of success, and to get there, you want to stay aligned to what's true for you. Make no compromises. Give yourself permission to do your business your way all the way.

If, after reading about this first Mindset, serving rings true for you, then serve. Make a conscious decision now that serving is the only way for you ahead.

And now, let us move on to the second mindset.

MINDSET TWO: ENABLE YOUR NEW IDENTITY TO EMERGE.

IF YOU ARE AN expert in your field, whatever your industry or line of work, you may subscribe to the belief that if you are not seen as that expert *at all times*, then you are compromising your identity and, subsequently, your credibility or reputation. In your mind, your identity lies almost exclusively within your expertise, and this is a trap.

This is what Malcolm Gladwell refers to as "the disadvantage of an advantage" in his book *David & Goliath*. He talks about how you can switch up the limitation that you see working against you into an advantage. For instance, you may believe that being an expert in architecture is a disadvantage in your role of attracting new clients to your firm, and Gladwell argues that this can actually be your very advantage. You have a unique perspective versus the trained salesperson in that position. You have hidden gifts that you can bring into the role because of your so-called "disadvantage."

In this section, we talk about this new perspective around your professional identity, one that actually serves your higher goals using your unique overall self.

What Is Your Professional Identity?

Your identity is how you define yourself in your business, profession, marketplace, and industry at large. When I ask the question, "What is your professional identity?" of my clients, there is often a pause.

We tend to think about—and define ourselves—mostly by what we *do*, rather than who we are *being* in our businesses or careers. We say things like: I run a dental office, I provide a service, I offer consulting, I help medical professionals, I coach HR managers, I operate a food truck business, etc., etc. If we do hear the "I am" statement, it is often followed by generic titles such as "I am a lawyer, I am a doctor, I am an accountant, I am a project manager."

These are tasks or titles, part of what you do, but *not* all of who you are. They are not your identity. You are the sum of all your experiences and exposures, all your credentials and qualifications, all your strengths and talents, and all your successes and failures.

Your Identity is Not Fixed in Stone

Here's the shocker: technical abilities cannot define the whole of you. They are simply a part of your overall identity.

We said earlier that your identity is unique because it's the sum of your gifts and talents, strengths and abilities, experiences and expertise. Your identity is thus ever-changing and it evolves as you grow into a better, wiser, and smarter version of yourself over time. Therefore, when you choose to increase your skills in, say, communications, influencing, negotiation, and sales, you are enriching your overall identity. You are neither compromising who you are, nor giving up one thing in order to gain another.

The Identity Crisis: How to Let Go of the Old to Evolve into the New

As you think about your own identity at this stage in your business, who do you see? Your answer to this question can explain how you show up in front of your employees, customers, partners, or peers. For example, if you primarily see yourself as a technical expert, even if you are the founder of your company now, ask yourself: Does this identity serve my highest interest in this role today? Does it fulfill all the "hats I need to wear" to do my job well and to move my business to the next level? If you moved from a purely technical role to that of a business owner or entrepreneur, the answer is a resounding NO!

One of my clients is a CTO of his company with his cofounder as the CEO. This CEO is the strategic brains behind the company, while my client focuses on the technical side of the house. Even in this situation, my client has to get involved in the grand vision, in the strategic direction of the company, and, to some extent, in the marketing and selling.

My client used to view this part of his job as being outside his strength and interest, and in a way, outside his real identity. As we probed into his mindset, he began to see his unique value contribution to this part of the business: a high-level strategic perspective featuring his analytical, logical, attention-to-detail approach, thanks to his background. He now feels good—note: indicator of serving!—about all the roles he plays in his business because he can see himself in a new light. This shift in identity also improved the relationship between the two co-founders.

If you run your own business, alone or with a cofounder, your primary identity must encompass your new responsibilities there. Still, it's perfectly normal to feel a "loss of identity" from being say an architect, engineer, code developer, or product creator to now playing the larger role of running a whole business.

Perceived loss of identity can gnaw at you at first, even if you choose to expand and grow as a person and professional. Amy Simpkins, one of my apprentices, experienced exactly this.

A brilliant MIT graduate and aerospace engineer with years of exciting space projects under her belt, Amy went through a huge identity crisis as she moved from her technical role at corporate toward becoming a life-architecting coach. Amy is beyond gifted and talented, and this new role suited her right brain perfectly, yet she felt a genuine sense of loss and grief during the transition. She struggled greatly with the "I am no longer a practicing engineer!" phase, even though she *is* still very much an engineer—even if she's not practicing the trade in a traditional sense, her engineer brain remains fully intact even in this new role.

What Amy came to see over time is that her identity did not *shrink* as she transitioned into a business coach; it expanded and grew more enriching. Because she is a business coach with a successful track record of engineering, she can relate to techie clients better than other business coaches who lack that particular brand of expertise. She applies her engineering side to all areas of her business as need be, because logical and analytical problem-solving skills can be applied to a world of possibilities outside of the aerospace industry.

And that lesson has paid off—today, Amy is the CEO of renewable energy consulting startup muGrid Analytics, with her husband as CTO, as well as a practicing business-strategy coach and mentor for female business starters.

The Loss, the Grief, the Discomfort of Shedding Old Identities

The familiarity with what we know is a bond so strong that many are never able to sever the cord. It matters not if the familiar stopped enabling their life goals or dreams long ago; it is still all they know. The known will always beat the unknown, and so they hold on to it with dear life.

Listen and you'll hear this phrase in many everyday conversations where we blatantly disqualify ourselves because "Well, that's not who I am, this is who I am!" This separation belief—*this*, not *that*— stops so much potential in this world. What if you could be whomever you decided? What if you could let go of an old identity in favor of a new and better one? What if you could expand your horizons and live and play from a much larger place?

You can.

You may feel some grief or a sense of loss and even discomfort at first. Say you'd always wanted to be a graphic designer, and you trained as one, worked as one, and then one day you find compelling reasons to pursue a new direction, say, to become a writer. Even if you knew in your heart and mind that this new direction is the right decision, aligned with your purpose in life, it is natural to feel a sense of loss of your identity as a graphic designer. That experience is still a part of you and always shall be, but moving forward, it won't be your *primary* identity.

Your identity will need to expand to encompass this new role of a writer as the center stage in the next phase of your profession. If you resist the necessary expansion of identity, if you hold on to the old identity and continue to see yourself as "*just* a graphic designer," you will sabotage yourself from reaching the full realm of possibilities awaiting you. Even if you do everything right with the physical and logistical transition to becoming a writer, your mind would still be over there, preoccupied with the old graphic designer identity, which no longer fits the new picture perfectly. Growth asks that you evolve into a new identity in order make room for expanded possibilities.

You Are Not What You Do

Your identity is not the same as your abilities to perform certain tasks. This is a point of confusion that may be worth clarifying. For instance, if you trained as ballet dancer, a part of your identity will always be "dancer"; however, it takes on different shapes. For instance, when you stop practicing, your skills will, over time, get rusty and you may not be able to perform the same tasks that you used to perform at the peak of your dancing career.

This is true for any vocation in life. You take them up for a certain period and you enjoy the fruits of your labor while engaging in those enriching activities, and then you move on. You may decide to return to ballet someday, and you'll have the advantage of familiarity and thus pick it up with more ease. But that's just *a part* of your ballet experience. The rest of it includes your understanding of the dance and the movements and the rhythms and the history behind it and the appreciation of performances and the art of teaching your craft to future ballet dancers and opening your own Ballet School if you choose to do so.

So, as you can see, you are not what you do. What you do is a part of who you are, and yet there is so much more to who you are as a result of every experience you've accumulated in your life. If you define the ballet dancer part of you as the person who performs the most complicated routines, then it would be hard to appreciate the other aspects that are also yours to claim.

Be Here Now

Having a really hard time letting go of the old identity? I hear you. We love our old stories. Who cares if they don't serve us anymore? Try and take them away and we are ready to go to war! Hence the dilemma of new directions in life. You are ready to embrace the new you, but your mind is not cooperating.

Let's trick it into cooperating, then.

My old yoga teacher could see my racing mind, and in yoga, being present is more important than doing the poses. Yoga is said to bring us to the beauty of the present moment, and I was missing the whole point in my rush to get to this pose and then the next one and so on. My mind, she said, is a wild, energetic puppy, and my only job is to get the puppy to come here, sit, and stay. If it took a hundred times to call the puppy, that's what it took. Come. Sit. Stay.

My puppy mind is doing much better these days, but our minds always love to get wrapped up in their old stories. Your old identities cannot survive without the running stories in your head. They depend on them. If you can interrupt the stories and stop the record from playing, you've got the upper hand in this game!

How do you do that? By training the puppy mind. By going into observation mode of your mind rather than participating in the chatter. By bringing your entire focus and attention to the present moment. Come. Sit. Stay. Repeat.

Next time you get a call from a prospect for your business, and your mind starts saying "Oh! You're just a coach! You're just an engineer!

You're not a salesperson!," all you need to do is calm the puppy mind and focus exclusively on what is happening right then and there. Do it a dozen times if you must. Interrupt the story over and over. Come to the present moment. Give your prospect the gift of your undivided attention. Deny access to the old records in your mind that feed your old identity. And you will gradually be more comfortable talking to your prospects without wrapping yourself up in those old identities and false stories about yourself. This is the work that gets you out of your own way, and helps you to evolve from old identities into new ones.

LIMITING BELIEF: "IF I GET GOOD AT SALES, I WON'T BE ABLE TO STAY TECHNICAL."

THIS LIMITING BELIEF IMPLIES that you can be one thing or another but not both. In mathematics, the Exclusive Or function is a logical operation that outputs true only when inputs differ (one is true, the other is false). The exclusive or function explicitly states "one or the other, but not neither nor both." This limiting belief, then, is what I call the Exclusive Or Dilemma. Somewhere, somehow, we got it in our heads that in a world where X and Y are vastly different areas of expertise, if we get great at X, we are then unable to also get great at Y.

Example: If you practice as an architect all your life and you are an expert in your field and you are great at what you do, and then all of a sudden you realize that you need expertise in sales and marketing, this limiting belief would see that pursuit as a compromise of skills. But is it possible to remain a highly accomplished architect and be great at selling and marketing? Are you capable of having both a technical brain and a business brain and doing both extremely well?

Well, let's explore. So you take pride and joy in your expertise. You enjoy your craft. You do great work and you proudly put your name on it. You likely get paid well for it. This works well as long as your total responsibility within the framework of your business or career is the showcase of this expertise.

The moment your roles and responsibilities expand, pause and re-evaluate. This expertise may still be useful, even critical to the success of your own business, but without other necessary skills for running a profitable, sustainable business, you will not survive for long. Agreed?

So as you can see, if you believe that getting great in other areas *compromises* your greatness in your current area, you are facing the exclusive or dilemma which I mentioned earlier: one or the other but not both. You are putting an illusional cap on your maximum possibilities in business and in life.

What It Means to Identify with Your Expert Self

Let's clarify what it means to identify with your expert self. I'll share a personal story:

I trained as an electrical engineer and earned both a bachelor and master of science at a top engineering school. Then I worked as an engineer for a few years. If you were to ask me about my identity, I'd say that a non-zero part of myself is still an engineer. It is my analytical, logical, problem solver, math-loving, techie, expert self.

But if you were to ask me now to apply my electrical engineering skills to a problem today, I would need a refresher course. Those skills have degraded over the years from lack of use, yet I am still capable of thinking and processing information like an engineer, especially in non-engineering applications.

So there is a distinction here to be made. When we talk about your expert self, we refer to the part of you that knows your field, has experienced it, and has a vast amount of knowledge in it. Whether you practice your craft daily to the fullest while running a business or have stepped away from it in order to focus elsewhere, the part of your identity that stems from your expertise is unchanged.

The same goes for your credibility. As a business owner, you will forever hold the credibility that your expertise and professional field afforded you, even if you stop practicing your craft. The choice to stay fully or partially in your field is one to make consciously, and it could be a different choice for each of us as we plan what we most want to do with our time and energy.

As you read on about Dominic Germana, Chief Engineer and Founder of Impact Embedded, a product-development consultancy in NC, you will find a "true engineer" who also turned entrepreneur. By this, I mean that he makes products with his bare hands; he creates instruments for doctors and gadgets for companies, and he gets involved in every stage of engineering a product. He also manages all aspects of his business, and does so quite successfully, while practicing his craft of engineering to the fullest. He had this to say on the topic: "People doing new and different things is what makes the world interesting. If everyone only ever did what they already knew how to do, then the world would be a boring place. Nothing novel would ever be developed if people were constrained by existing knowledge and experience."

Dominic has wanted to stay extremely technical while still developing skills in marketing, branding, and selling his services. He has expanded his old engineer identity to encompass many additional areas of expertise in order to fulfill his new expanded role as a technical business owner, and he could not be happier about it. Dominic summarized this by saying, "You can achieve the balance of technical vs. non-technical contributions that you desire in your business; you just have to be intentional about it."

So, if you truly LOVE the technical side of the work, and you want to continue spending time and energy doing that in your business, even as the owner or founder, all the more power to you. The takeaway here is to highlight your real desires and drives for work and then create the right business model around it. You are not boxed into a technical role, a business management role, or any role for that matter, regardless of your education or past experience. You have a choice! As Dominic has demonstrated, it is entirely possible to be a true engineer and still run your own company.

Make A Pledge: I Will Stay True to Who I Am!

Some of us have no choice but to be in business for ourselves. Sure, we could go get a job, but we won't. We simply can't NOT do this: be our own boss, run our own company, call our own shots. We have to make this work. We Just Have To.

To do this, you have to stay true to who you are while running your own successful and profitable business. Why? Because if you feel you have to give up a part of your core, your essence, your true self, in order to become a profitable business owner, you might as well go back and get a job. Compromise of values is one of the top reasons most of us left our jobs in favor of our own ventures, so that we could be true to who we are, and what we are about, and still do our great work in this world.

GUIDING PRINCIPLE: YOUR EXPANDED IDENTITY CLEARS THE WAY TO YOUR PROFITABLE BUSINESS

When you allow your identity to expand, it can encompass all your expertise and experiences, including new skills such as sales, communication, leadership, management, and whatever else you need to run a tight ship and be on your way to a sustainable, profitable business. You can know all this, excel at it all, and still be one person with one identity, because all these building blocks of your expanded identity integrate and work well together. You are able to seamlessly go through them because that's what it means to expand and enrich the sum of who you are. It's like learning multiple languages. You study for years, but then one day, they all assimilate in your head and out comes the language you call forth. You don't think "Oh wait, now I have to speak German." You simply do it. It's your mind's instant response to the situation at hand, and learning those new languages did not "take away" your ability to speak your mother tongue.

If you learn to look at your new identity in the right way, it can be your ultimate competitive advantage, not because nobody else has similar skills—they sure do—but because of the right mindset here. The advantage comes when you are able to embrace the technical side, the part that may have been your single preferred identity in the past, as well as your business side, some of which you may have resisted until recently. With the new mindset, the whole is greater than the sum of its parts, as long as you know how to position yourself and see this combined value with confidence.

See, your new mindset would encourage you to believe that you can be a technical expert in your field and a powerful communicator, negotiator, and salesperson, so there would be no need to apologize for it, as most professionals do: "I'm sorry, but I'm not really technical." Or, "I'm sorry, but I'm not really a salesperson." This pathetic apology accomplishes one thing and one thing only: It diminishes you as a professional in the eyes of your prospect (which is a shame, because that's not fair to you at all!) You may feel that you are being humble, but instead, you are sabotaging your chances of seizing an opportunity by pushing your prospect away as you highlight a delusional inability on your part.

Think about it: A technical genius apologizes to me for not being a salesperson and basically lacking business savvy, but still wants me to buy her product. Why would I be *more attracted* to buy from her if she just admitted that she is "only a techie"? How can she earn my respect if she basically doesn't know how to run a business? Will she apologize for invoicing me incorrectly or not receiving my payments or not scheduling my calls right? A myriad of concerns fills my head, because what I hear from her is this: You should expect nothing but technical expertise from our business relationship! And I will walk away as fast as possible and go buy from someone else, who may be less of a techie genius but who has more professional business savvy.

So stop labeling yourself and apologizing for it. It serves no one. Instead, choose to develop the competitive advantage muscle: expand your very necessary selling skills by learning to serve your customers, while still leveraging your technical side in your positioning.

MINDSET THREE: CARE ABOUT YOUR PROSPECTS AND SHOW IT.

NOTE THAT WE ARE talking prospects, not customers. This is not about great customer service. A prospect has not yet bought from you. They are not your customer yet and there is no certainty that they will become your customer later. This is precisely when you start caring about them.

During a coaching session with one of my clients, he was recounting a meeting with a prospect. He is in the IT service-provider business, and with his highly technical background, he brings lots of passion to the field with his techie, geeky side. At the meeting, he shared how his solution is the perfect answer for their problems, how every feature in his offering can be relevant to their challenges. He went into great detail to articulate these points.

I asked him if he had also remembered to show this prospect how much he *cares* about them, their mission, their company's vision and direction, and about solving their challenge and being of service to them. "Hmmm. What do you mean?" my client asked.

Vocalizing that you care, rather than implying it, is the distinction here. Should it not be enough that you did your due diligence by digging into their problems and challenges and then telling them about your brilliant solution, you wonder? Is it not obvious that you care by showing up, listening, taking notes, answering questions, and being willing to work with them, you ask?

Maybe. It may be enough if they need the solution right away. It may be enough to get them to sign a minimal contract or to casually agree to do business with you. It may be enough to move forward with you, even if reluctantly, because they can't stand your competitor. In other words, it may be enough to get some business, yes.

But are you here to get a reluctant yes when you could get an unequivocal one instead? To set yourself apart, you want to raise the bar on how a business partnership with you can revolutionize their business and transform their future. You want to arrive at an absolute YES and cultivate a relationship based on mutual trust and a powerful connection. And a reluctant yes is a poor start to any such relationship.

You can only achieve those two gems—mutual trust and a powerful connection—when you care *and* when they know how much you care.

Caring about your prospects and demonstrating this care will take everything you are doing to a new level and give you a rare competitive edge. When you care more, you don't just successfully close more business; you close more business with the type of customer who shares your values of trust, care, and integrity, because you put trust before transaction, care before consumption, people first and business second. These customers generate more than mere revenue for your business—they become your raving fans. They stay with you longer. They refer you. They boost your brand. They do your marketing *for* you, in a way. They make doing business truly joyful, all because of an upfront investment you made by showing them how much you care about them as people.

When we care deeply about someone who is not even a customer or client yet, we are serving, and something magical happens when you do this. The human side emerges. Conversations flow with ease. Trust forms. Sales becomes an organic outcome. Putting people before business makes doing business with people so much more effortless.

Caring about the Prospect: How to Show It

Let's take a closer look at yourself first. How do you think you come across to others, and how accurate is that perception?

A client of mine earlier expressed his care by way of sharing his technical skills and expertise. He gave of his knowledge freely, answered questions, and transferred information that could prove useful to his prospects. He leveraged his comfort zone, his technical expertise, and the language of technology, in hopes that it relayed the message of care.

But what if the prospect had very little technical savvy, and far less appreciation for technology than my client, and needed to hear in simpler terms that my client understood his concerns, and that he really could allay his fears and frustrations and truly support them in this transition to a new IT provider? What if the prospect needed to hear that my client cares in his language, and thus never picked up the good intentions of my client because of his more technical, analytical, matter-of-fact verbiage?

What a missed opportunity! The intentions of both parties are very good, but each is operating at a different frequency. They speak a slightly different language. They understand each other, as one would understand someone who speaks one's own language poorly, which may be good enough, but neither deep nor powerful. So much is lost, as we well know, in translation.

What should my client have done instead? How could we remove the need for *any* translation by clearly communicating that we understand and we care?

Adapt Your Style to Theirs

We will borrow a chapter from the work of Dr. Steven Covey, an American author, speaker, and educator who transformed the idea of success through his work *The Seven Habits of Highly Effective People*. The most relevant habit to our point here is his Habit 5: Seek First to Understand, then to Be Understood. This notion is at the cornerstone of serving, whereby we start creating a connection with our prospects through deep understanding before presenting our own ideas and asking them to now understand our position. Seeking to understand takes the form of asking questions, being curious, deep listening, and observing our prospect. We do this at first because it allows us to quickly assess whether they respond well to our style and preferences in communication. When that is the case, we can continue in the same mode. But when that's not the case, we need to adapt our approach. The goal is not merely to communicate, but to connect.

"Everyone communicates but few connect."
—John Maxwell

What does it mean to connect? It means to have the full attention and interest of the person with whom you are interacting in the most effortless way possible. To do this, we need to adapt to their style, rather than stick to ours.

I teach my clients to look for certain signs to pick up on the style of an individual. Here are examples of some critical signs to look for:

- Is this person more outgoing or reserved?
- Does this person speak faster or slower than me?
- Does this person think high-level or prefer intricate details?
- Does this person value end-results more or less than the process?

As you observe your prospect, whether it be on the phone or in person, you can quickly learn where they fall in these preferences. This can give you a quick framework as to how you should best adapt your style to connect with them, since you already know well where you fall with your preferences.

Mirror Their Tone, Energy, and Style

To have the highest level of impact and to be able to connect with the person in front of you in the deepest way possible, these three components—your energy, your pace, and your style—must mirror that of your prospect as closely as possible.

If you are a fast talker and your prospect is more measured in their pace, slow down and adapt to their pace. If you are highly enthusiastic, and your prospect is more on the passive or serious scale, tone down your enthusiasm slightly. If you bring a lot of energy into the call, and your prospect is more even, adjust your level while still energizing the conversation. If they are tentative and unsure, ask permission before you move to the next step in the conversation and gently bring them along. If they want a strategic high-level solution, skip the details and stay high-level with them until they show interest in the nitty-gritty. If you hear emphasis on results, focus on the specific results that you help them create, but if they're more interested in your process or methodology, feel free to elaborate on those. You get the picture.

Now, you may believe your high energy, your enthusiasm, and your fast pace are your greatest assets, or that your quiet nature, your captive listening, and your measured pace may be your strengths. They are and they can indeed serve you well in many circumstances. However, if a deep connection to another human being is your priority here, you need to prioritize *their* comfort zone over *yours* by adapting your style. This is a choice. You don't have to do any of this . . . but you can connect a lot better every single time you choose to do it.

By adapting your energy, style, and pace to your prospect, you can help them relate to you and feel that you truly get them, which you now would. You will then easily build trust, create a bond, and cultivate a safe space for your prospect to share their fears and frustrations. You are not in the conversation to impress. You are in the conversation to serve, and I don't know about you, but I'm more willing to adapt every time to gain a fraction of those rewards.

(If you're interested in learning more about creating deep connections, the best resource is learning DiSC Behavior Profiling, as well as the work of Merrick Rosenberg in both of his books, *Taking Flight* and *The Chameleon*.)

Adapting to your prospect's style of communication is the most effective and effortless and non-verbal way to show that you care, and it is a true competitive edge as very, VERY few business owners and entrepreneurs are even aware of this concept, much less knowledgeable about how to use it.

Identify Values Quickly

Values are those ideals and principles that one holds very near and dear. Yours are not necessarily the same as mine or those of your prospect. To simplify values, I like to categorize them into non-negotiable values and preferred values. You may adjust your preferred values based on the overall situation; you would not do so with the non-negotiable ones.

Example: One of my preferred values is responsiveness; and when I interact with someone who lacks this value, I have to think very hard about whether to continue the relationship. Yet, at times, the benefits of the overall relationship outweighs my desire for a high level of responsiveness, and I'm happy to exercise flexibility here.

This decision has served me well. You learn, for example, that some people are very brief in their responses, communicate at an absolute minimum, and may go weeks without answering your question. This awareness was essential in helping me create a healthy relationship with my clients who leaned this way. I know, for instance, that John will not be replying to my email, unless it's urgent for him, and that has nothing to do with his view on our coaching relationship. In fact, not hearing from John except during our sessions is perfectly normal. On the other hand, if I go two weeks without hearing from my highly responsive client, I check in with her, knowing full well that she values the gesture.

Now, one of my non-negotiable values in a client is total commitment to their own growth and to the coaching process. I'm not willing to compromise on this one because I've learned from past mistakes that it does not serve them. A so-so commitment directly affects their success in the coaching. I want my clients to be rock stars, and for that possibility, we need the right timing and a high level of desire for results before we enter into a coaching agreement together. When the total commitment is in place, people make the seemingly impossible happen, and when you see your non-negotiable values in action, you understand why it's important to stick to them!

In the end, the idea here is to connect with someone on a shared value and thus use it to deepen the relationship. When you find out, for instance, that your prospect highly values testimonials of past clients before hiring you, you can appreciate that and accommodate them. This is more than just agreeing to provide a list of your past clients who are willing to endorse you; it's articulating your understanding of how important this is to them. You may say something like, "You know, Suzie, I'm so glad you asked for referrals on my work. I also value strong endorsements and a proven track record before I hire someone for my own company. Let me see how I can accommodate that for you."

So as you adapt your style in the process above, listen for your prospect's values, and speak to them. Acknowledge them. Show that you care by genuinely connecting on those values. Then observe how your prospect's demeanor toward you improves. You can often see them relaxing and opening up more. You can hear the trust building up in their voice, and in their body language if you happen to be in person. You may even see them lean in to you, a gesture of trust and connection. When you feel this connection, the magic starts to happen.

Tell the Truth

If you haven't read *On Writing* by Stephen King, stop reading my book this minute and go do that now. It's the most exquisite memoir on writing and on life. My favorite quote by King is this:

"Now comes the big question: What are you going to write about? And the equally big answer: Anything you damn well want. Anything at all . . . as long as you tell the truth."

And that is precisely what we have the obligation to do in our businesses, in our craft, and in our relationships. Tell the truth. That is the deepest expression of caring, as long as it is delivered with utmost honesty and sincerity. Our job with serving is to tell the truth. Our job is not to impress potential clients and customers. Our job is not to coerce them to work with us. Our job is not to worry if they will like us. Our job is to tell the truth, gently but firmly, clearly and confidently, with permission but without apology. That is being of true service, and this is a skill that you *can* develop.

Here is how this may go over in a dialogue in which we have to tell John something that his best friend would likely not dare tell him:

You: John, would it be ok if I shared my observations with you?

John: Ok, sure.

You: From what you have shared, I don't believe you have a strategy issue here. Rather, you are not yet 100% committed to the outcomes you mentioned.

John: Of course I'm committed. I've done XYZ. I'm doing the best I can. Why would you say that?

You: I hear you, and I agree you are *somewhat* committed, but when you are 100% committed, nothing gets in the way. Think of your commitment to be at work on Monday morning at nine a.m. Emergencies notwithstanding, you know you'll be there. That's 100% commitment. Can you say you have that level of commitment to this goal, John?

John: Hmmm. Not sure. How would I know?

You: You would know when this goal becomes certain in your mind as having already happened, similar to showing up at the office at nine. Strategy is irrelevant right now. First, you have to decide on the outcome. What is your level of desire for this goal?

What competing priorities may get in the way? What needs to happen for you to reach 100% commitment to this goal?

Think about it. When you have a meeting or a flight or a child pickup, you already know in your mind that the event will happen with your full participation. If need be, you will scramble and hurry, but it will happen. In your mind, the meeting, the flight, or the child pickup is not just something you want; it is a non-negotiable outcome in your schedule that day. You are 100% committed to making it happen. When you see your goals in that light, when you are certain that they are going to happen, something shifts. You operate from a different place—a powerful, knowing, and certain place. That's what it means to be 100% committed. Then you can figure out the strategy to get there.

LIMITING BELIEF: "I'M NOT GOOD WITH PEOPLE. I'M AN INTROVERT. I'M SHY. I'M X."

THERE IS NO SUCH thing as "not good with people." It is a self-inflicted label. It is a false, made-up story to disqualify yourself. It is an attack on your self-esteem. You might as well punch yourself in the face every time you say it.

You are a person. You are connected to others. You cannot *not* be good with people. It is not how you are with people that is the problem; it's how you think about it and what you then say to yourself about it that creates all the problems you are experiencing.

You are with people in your own way, just as everyone else is, because, thankfully, there is no one way to be. It's your mind that groups everyone else into "good with people" and "not good with people" groups and creates this cruel separation between you and others, your abilities and theirs. It's an illusion.

So you can safely throw the words "not good with people" out of your vocabulary. Discard them forever. You are GREAT with people by the virtue of the fact that you are one of them. You may choose not to exercise this great ability but you do have it. You own it and you can't disown it.

With that in mind, remember, as we've shared before, the story. Your mind always wants you to believe a story. What is your story behind being "not good with people"?

Maybe at some point in your life, in college or your first year at work, you had an experience. You may have felt awkward in a setting with new people. You may have had to go to a "networking" event, and if you think you are bad at those, I have news for you. The extroverts among us detest networking events, too. But one way or another, you surmised that you are not good with people based on a handful of similar and, according to you, negative experiences. Then you came up with "I am" labels to put those experiences into "facts," And the label stuck.

Perhaps you're even secretly happy with this situation. It gives you a get-out-of-jail-free card. You're not good with people, so you can skip the phone conversation with your prospect and hide behind email. You're not good with people, so you're going to send your sales guy to the customer site, even if they really need to talk to the owner. You're not good with people, so you will not participate in a crucial conversation, because that's not your forte.

The Advantages of Your Weaknesses

A weakness is not a bad thing. A weakness can be your greatest asset if you know how to leverage it. Being an introvert is not only a great thing, it can be your foremost strength, so please stop using it as an excuse for weakness.

(That request goes for every weakness with which you've labeled yourself, but back to introversion.)

"I'm an introvert," you say. OK. So? How is that making the case for not connecting with your prospects in a way that shows you really care about them?

Introverts close large deals every day. Introverts run profitable, successful businesses and interact with other people every day. Introverts have conversations, even if in their own style, come up with innovative ideas worth lots of money, create clients, and get signed contracts every day.

The introverts who do this choose not to see their approach and style as a hindrance. Microsoft's founder, Bill Gates, views himself as a "solitary introvert," and this has only contributed to his massive success. In his own words, "If you're clever, you can learn to get the benefits of being an introvert, which might be, say, being willing to go off for a few days and think about a tough problem, read everything you can, push yourself very hard to think out on the edge of that area."

Among the other well-known introverts who've done extremely well for themselves are Warren Buffett, Larry Page, and Elon Musk. Choose to see your introvert tendencies as a great gift!

What would happen to your business if you saw your being an introvert as a true strength, and felt no pressure to change it in order to attract your ideal customers and clients?

If your mind brings up the image of the zealous salesperson doing his work and running from one high-energy meeting to another, I don't blame you. That is a turn-off, and that is not what serving is about.

You are here to create a business in your own way and according to your own style. You can stay true to your introvert tendencies and still learn to serve and create an amazing business. If your style is a more quiet, reserved, methodical, and measured way, then honor that. The question, then, isn't how to *overcome* being an introvert in order to engage with people, because that would be like asking you to change your very essence—no wonder you resist it. The real question is, how can you turn being an introvert into a true advantage when you engage people?

The answer is in adapting your style.

As an introvert, you are likely more reserved and prefer to listen more than to lead conversations. Your prospect would really appreciate this if they prefer to do the talking and being heard. So if the style of your prospect is more outgoing and talkative, your introvert nature suits them. Where you may need to adapt is to be sensitive to their faster pace and adjust yours so you connect better, or you may need to be more engaged and outwardly confident and show this in your tone of voice and posture. These simple changes can go very far when you connect with someone who is the opposite style, and yet none of them take away from your natural essence of being an introvert.

How is being an introvert an advantage, then? Well, you are a keen observer of people. You take more in. You listen well. You process and understand at a deeper level, and so on. As you bring those qualities into your relationships, while adapting as necessary, you create a deep level of trust and make it easier to want to do business with you.

You cannot run a healthy, sustainable, profitable, and fulfilling business and *not* interact with people. You cannot escape this non-negotiable, not if you want the vision, the dream, and the long-term impact of your business.

I have had clients who tried to use this introversion excuse to get out of calling a prospect or having a powerful conversation, but I do not allow them to disqualify themselves so. I challenge them, as I do you, to really hear yourself as you use these false labels. When have they ever served you? How many missed opportunities have they brought you? How much longer will you allow the label to control you?

Because of this story, which you have convinced yourself and believed for so long, you may have avoided excellent opportunities to engage and interact with people. You may be out of practice in relating and conversing and creating connections with people. You may be very uncomfortable at the idea of having conversations or building relationships. Bringing this to light can help you take the first step toward positive change.

Play a Game to Prove Your Story Wrong

Here's a game to prove that you are indeed GREAT with people. Ask a friend to participate here. Tell your friend that you will give him or her $1,000 in cash if you don't make a call to a prospect and have an hour-long conversation. Make a bet. Shake hands on it.

Now, is it possible that this idea, this so-called "fact" that you're "not good with people" would even enter your mind? Not possible. Not when

$1,000 in cash is at risk. You'd find a way to be good enough with people to talk for an hour, I'm sure.

How is it possible, then, to dismantle a "fact" with just a few dollars? Facts should withstand a lot more than that. The fact that you cannot fly if you jump out of a window does not alter, no matter how much money is on the line or how motivated you might be to fly. But this "I'm not good with people" story is a false, unfounded limiting belief, and one that you can now release with a simple game.

So, now that you know you are good—even great—with people, you are ready to integrate the mindset in question: to show that you care about your prospects and to demonstrate this care. Everything we talked about earlier is within your reach. You are entirely capable of building trust, having deep, meaningful conversations with prospects, appearing confident and curious, and creating a competitive edge for yourself.

Imagine the possibilities in a world where you are great with people. They're endless.

Understand the Problem First

You are in business because you have something to offer, and this thing you have—a product or a service or a combination—is the answer to a problem. Your product or service solves this problem, and if you want people to buy your solution, you need to help them see that you can solve this particular problem for them.

This problem that your business is solving may be simple, like making a lotion for dry skin or a hydrating drink for athletes, or it may be complex, like a comprehensive IT solution for a fifty-person organization, complete with the latest technology. In every case, your first task is to identify whether your prospect is the right candidate for your solution. To do this, you need to learn more about them—a lot more! You need to become an expert on their problems, their frustrations, and their challenges. You first need to be able to explain their situation *better* than they can explain it.

When you can do this, your solution will sell itself.

The precise timing of presenting your offer is no small detail; the worst mistake you can make is to rush to your brilliant solution and push it onto a prospect *before* you have fully and completely understood the problem. This skill alone is so rare that you can bet it will set you apart from your competitors once you master it.

So, remember, this initial process is not about you or your solution. It is entirely about your prospect and their problem. Your solution is your zone of genius, the zone where you do your best work, but first, focus on fully and completely understanding the problem. Slow down, be curious, ask more questions to best grasp the problem until you are certain that your solution is the ideal answer. You are first and foremost a vessel of inquiry, education, and information as you determine (A) whether your prospect needs what you have, and (B) whether you are the right person to solve it for them. If so, you then, with permission, may proceed to tell them all about it, and if not? Then tell them the truth and suggest other resources that may be a better fit. Always serve their interests above yours.

As you put the focus and attention on your prospect, you will feel less self-conscious and more confident. What you may have perceived as "pitching" morphs into a caring conversation to explore options. When you are 100% focused on them, your shyness or awkwardness in interacting with them begins to dissolve because the spotlight is no longer on you.

GUIDING PRINCIPLE: INFUSE YOUR CURIOSITY WITH EMPATHY

How do we effectively shift the spotlight over to our prospect, then? We call on abilities that are inherent to us all: our curiosity and our empathy.

Curiosity: a strong desire to know or learn something.

Empathy: the ability to understand and share the feelings of another.

Curiosity alone is good, but when you infuse it with empathy, you go from good to great. Let's demonstrate this now.

Curiosity *without* empathy would sound like this:

"John, so your network went down yesterday afternoon and the team lost five hours of productivity. Tell me, please: What exactly did you do after your network went down? What steps did you follow?"

Curiosity *infused with* empathy would sound like this:

"John, I can imagine that you were frustrated when your network went down during high-traffic time and it probably caused a lot of doubt and angst with the loss in productivity. What an inconvenience! Listen, I'm curious what steps you took after the outage? This would help me better understand your procedures so I can help prevent this from happening again."

With a few words, you can raise the impact of your words. Not only will empathy tell this prospect that you care and understand, it will make a marked difference between a decision to work with you or pass on your offer. When your prospect can feel that you care and can see that you are also the expert they have been looking for, they will be a lot more likely to move forward with you.

This empathy piece is often missing when you are too focused on solving the problem right away, and, while you have the best intentions, the prospect may still need to hear that you care before getting down to work. Empathy may be one of *their* non-negotiable values in doing business with you, or it may be what has been missing in their business dealings all along, and they crave it without knowing it. Either way, empathy will only help you come across as a professional and a human being. Show empathy. You will only raise the bar on your own professionalism and attract the higher caliber of clients your way.

I would even argue that showing empathy in a genuine way pays higher dividends than securing additional qualifications, certifications, or industry awards. At the end of the day, you are dealing with people. Businesses are made up of people, and people care little how many acronyms follow your name so long as you can solve their business problem and care about them as people. What matters most is the *quality* of your relationships with people, which has a lot to do with your ability to express empathy and curiosity.

In all my years of coaching executives, leaders, business owners, and career professionals, I have not *once* been asked about my "coaching certification."

(I put that in quotes because there is no official certification for coaching; there are organizations and recommendations, that's all!)

No, my clients care only if I can help them with their problem, so I chose not to pursue a coaching certification for two reasons. One, I was never able to see the ROI on the hard-earned industry certifications I achieved at Cisco, and two, the best coaches in the world, whom I had come to respect, were not formally certified. So, I took a chance. I opted for an autonomous and creative approach to establishing my coaching practice.

The results? Beyond my wildest expectations. It still astounds me what people truly care about, how effortlessly you can be of service and secure business, and how much you learn and grow in the process of direct experience versus the path of getting certified or accredited by this and that organization. Now, don't get me wrong—I have invested tens of thousands of dollars in private coaches and other resources to educate myself, and constant learning is an invaluable asset that I cherish, but I attribute the success of my coaching business to (1) being really good at what I do, (2) doing my work with empathy, curiosity, and a high level of professionalism, and (3) the ability to connect and relate to people, all of which I'm sharing with you here in this book.

How to Show Empathy

"People won't care how much you know until they know how much you care." This favorite quote been repeated so often that we know it as a well-known truism. So how can you raise the bar on your empathy? How can you ask your questions and show empathy for what your prospect is experiencing?

You are not dealing with consumers of the 1980s anymore. Your buyers are human beings, and they are more educated and informed and selective than ever before. They can find out everything they want about you and your product before ever speaking to you. They can look up all the news on your company, and all that has been said about you on social media. They are not just buying a commodity today; they are buying a why, a belief, a cause, and they want to know why they should choose you. They are not price shopping for the best deal in town; they want a deeper reason to do business with you. The consumer of today is helping you build the companies and businesses of tomorrow, and the business that is truly aligned to their values speaks the loudest. As the options increase in every market for the consumer, the way to set yourself apart is to be more authentic.

Authenticity does not ask that you have the coolest product with the most features or the lowest-priced service or the fastest delivery method. Authenticity doesn't care about your social media following or your Likes or Comments. Authenticity isn't interested in your credentials or certifications or awards; those are great to have, but far from necessary for being authentic.

The simplest way to be authentic is to care, and to demonstrate this care in unmistakable ways and in every opportunity possible. Care in the most genuine and honest way you know how. Care in a way that comes from place of true service, our first mindset, and care without attachment to closing the deal or making a sale. Care unconditionally and enter an empathetic state of mind when you are with your prospect. All you have to do is to be right here and right now with the person in front of you, but let's define what that means in more tangible terms:

1. Be Fully Present in Every Interaction and Conversation

When you are fully present with the prospect, you are not thinking ahead about how you would respond and not thinking back about similar conversations in the past and how they unfolded. When you are present without labeling everything in your mind, you offer a rare gift: 100% of your attention and focus, an experience for which people are hungry in our fast-paced, multitasking world. This comes before doing business. This tuning in and deep listening is the foundation of being right here and right now.

Total presence is the greatest gift you can offer. Being present means setting aside the noise and chatter in your mind in order to create space. It means taking a deep breath, grounding your body (whether seated or standing), facing the person speaking to you, hearing them, and responding in kind without saying much. Let your posture and body language—your eyes, your energy, your gestures—emanate presence so that your voice doesn't have to fill the air.

Don't believe the impact? Do this in the very next conversation with anyone you are having, including a family member or partner, and watch the response. Look for subtle cues in their body, their tone of voice, their pace, and their level of listening back when you begin to speak. Look for the appreciation and the presence they bring to the conversation in return.

2. Come From a Place of Genuine Curiosity

Practice genuine curiosity in your approach next time you connect with another person. Let's say you meet a new prospect today and want to connect with them. Instead of just exchanging a few pleasantries about the weather or talking about yourself, ask them about their big dream and what's important to them now and why? If they start to talk about a challenge, ask them what would they like to have happen with that situation, and what support they may need along the way? Listen. Get curious. Ask them to tell you more.

You're not there to solve their problem or to offer advice. Not yet. You're there to be a curious, engaged, active listener. You are inviting them to be heard by creating a safe space, even if just for a few minutes. Perhaps you are the only one doing that for them. Practice this with at least one stranger and one close friend or family member before practicing it with a prospect, and observe how this act of engaging deeper with another makes YOU feel. Test how far your curiosity can take you and how much they open up to you in return. Let how you feel guide you deeper into empathy for others.

3. Challenge Your Own Opinions and Judgments

Your beliefs and values drive your decisions in life. But what if you challenged them for a change? This simply means to question your beliefs and see matters from the other point of view, to take the opposite side of the argument than you normally would and defend that position. That's what we're doing in this book with mindset shifts, so why not bring it into every conversation?

Here's my vulnerable personal example: I'm ashamed to admit that I used to believe suicide to be a purely selfish act. *How can anyone do that to the loved ones they leave behind?* I thought. But after Robin Williams committed suicide in 2014, I felt devastated, and then I started to learn more about suicide and to question my own preconceived notions.

I am grateful that I was able to turn around my limiting beliefs, and today, I truly see suicide as a desperate cry for help. It makes me more empathetic about mental illness and more encouraging that those who suffer from it get help. You don't know what you might learn if you set aside your beliefs long enough to hear another viewpoint or to explore deeper as to why you even believe what you believe in the first place.

4. Use Empathy Language in a Conversation

Listening deeply and completely is a wonderful skill to start with, but so is knowing what to say—or not to say—in response. Here are some phrases I find useful and genuine when someone like a friend or a client is confiding in me:

- "I can't imagine what that's like. Please tell me more."
- "I'd love to help. What specifically would help you in this situation?"

- "If you could have anything right now to move past this phase (in your business or your life), what would it be?"

Stay clear of judging, sharing similar experiences ("Same thing happened to me!" or "Oh, I know!"), pointing out flaws, or jumping in to solve the problem. Practice the right words, the right phrases, and say them naturally.

If you forget everything else, remember what the Dalai Lama said about love: "What is Love? Love is the *absence* of judgment." That is the deepest and highest form of empathy. Empathy is an act of love, and yes, it is appropriate to bring love into business conversations with potential future clients.

Four Practical Ways to Increase How Much You Care

What are some tangible ways to demonstrate our deep care for prospects? Here are my four proven ways:

1. Ask Them What They Most Care About if They Were to Engage with You

That's right. Simply ask your prospect what they most care about. Phrase it just like that: "Clara, it's really good to meet you and to get to know you better. I'd love to start off by asking you what you most care about in engaging a new consultant on this project? What's most important to you here?"

Some clients may care about punctual responses and others may care about methods and procedures. Some may want email communication and others may always prefer a phone call. These may seem like small details to you, but not so much to them. The more you know about what *they* care about, the more easily and appropriately you can relate to and connect with them.

2. Listen and Validate What You Heard by Repeating and Paraphrasing

This is a simple communication concept, but few actually do it well. In the conversation, be completely present and focused on what your prospect is telling you. Even if you are totally off topic, and they're sharing some horror story about their last IT person or their frustrations about the system, it is your job to listen and to make them feel heard before proceeding to solve the problem. You need to do this delicately and tactfully. One example of how you might phrase it is: "You know, Melissa, I know you had a poor experience with your last IT person, and I can see how you would be worried about hiring someone new. I also hear your doubts about not knowing exactly what next step to take, which can be a scary place to be in business. Did I understand your concerns correctly here? Did I miss anything?"

And after they validate your understanding, you can add, "Great. Would it be okay if I share some ideas on how I can help you with all of this?"

3. Treat Oversights and Mistakes as Golden Opportunities

When it has happened that I totally forgot about a scheduled call due to jet lag or time zone mix-ups—an oversight on my part, in other words—I have gladly gone the extra mile to make it up to the prospect. Note that this is not an existing client, but a prospect, someone who had inquired about my services. I'd make it up by scheduling a two-hour call, giving them an extra hour of my time. Even if they say no, I show how much I care and, as a professional, how much I regret my oversight.

If you had an oversight of, say, misquoting the prospect on your project or double-booking on your availability, go back and be transparent. "Pete, I gotta tell you, I feel really bad about double-booking you when I said I can start you in September. My oversight. I want to make it up to you because it's important for me to earn your trust before doing business with you. Might we perhaps renegotiate the start date and I'm willing to do [X] on top to show you how much I care about earning your business?"

4. Be Willing to Turn Them Away if Your Service is Not 100% Right for Them at this Time

This is what we must do when we come from a place of true service. I have taught my clients to do this as they adopt the mindset of service over selling. Still, it gets tricky to say no to business, so be careful with this one.

On one occasion, one of my prospects even confided in me that she had up to $10,000 set aside and wanted to work with me. But she was brand-new to starting her business, and for her to maximize her investment with me, she'd have had to be further along. So, in service to her, I suggested one of my self-paced online courses for business owners before we could engage her in private coaching.

Caring means you place the interests of your customer before your own. This act of kindness says that you are highly selective in doing business with only those whom you can completely serve, and if that element is not in place, then you would not be creating a win-win for all parties if you went ahead.

You are allowed to turn away business that does not meet your criteria 100% and to be completely transparent with your prospects. To take this caring one step further, you can offer to find them the right service provider or connect them with a resource until such time that your services might be right for them. This is the highest act of caring, and what emerges from operating this way never ceases to surprise me. In one case, a prospect came back to me three years later, when it made perfect sense for us to engage, and signed a much larger contract than I could even have imagined proposing at the earlier time.

So saying NO to a less-than-ideal opportunity leaves you open to saying YES to more-ideal opportunities. And this is how you can step higher and higher onto the ladder of success—you have to say NO to so-so opportunities in order to make room for the right ones.

Caring is big. Caring goes far and deep. Caring is the deposit you make in a prospect's bank account, which over time earns you dividends of trust, reciprocity, and future business, not to mention unforeseen opportunities.

When you do this part well, you will create a sustainable, healthy edge for your business without having to slash your prices or be the best game in town. When you care and show it well and do it consistently, you will create opportunities beyond your grasp.

MINDSET FOUR: CHARGE APPROPRIATELY FOR YOUR SERVICES.

Most business owners come from a place of generosity, humility, and goodwill by pricing their services or products "affordably," which is often way lower than their competitors. They want their prospective buyers to see how unselfishly they are running their business and how much of a "better deal" they are getting by working with them versus someone else.

Except it doesn't work that way. Your underpricing yourself does nobody a favor—not you, not your prospects, not even your competitors. This is the beginning of confusion for most business owners because it's another paradox. It doesn't make much logical sense.

My mastermind group was just as keen to explore and research this Abundant Sales Mindset as was I. Our research around this led us to new discoveries every time and left us surprised as to the counterintuitive nature of them. When we started out as coaches, for example, we priced ourselves as low as possible. We wanted to be kind and generous. We wanted to be affordable and accessible to everybody. We wanted to make money at any cost. And we struggled selling our tiny $250 or $375 packages. We struggled to convince our prospects that the value of such a package could be as much as 100 times the investment. Why? Because they didn't believe us. We were priced way too low. They could not believe that $250 could possibly get them a $10,000 raise in salary or a $20,000 signing bonus or a $30,000 client contract.

The Ultimate Punishment for Your Low Prices

I met up with one of my favorite yoga teachers in Los Angeles a while ago, and when she shared this particular client story, my jaw dropped, so I begged her to let me put it in my book. "As long as it's anonymous," she agreed. So, here it is:

A client took a couple of private sessions with her for his shoulder pain. He did not know how much she charged, nor did he care. He felt incredible afterwards. The sessions had an immediate positive impact on his body. Later, he had his assistant call in to pay the invoice. (Yep, he was that kind of well-to-do client with his own PA to do his bidding! Nice, right?)

The assistant inquired about additional ongoing private sessions, which the boss wanted to do, but after my friend quoted her rates, she came back with this shocking statement: "He doesn't want to do any more sessions. He doesn't believe you can be that good if your prices are that low. Sorry!"

It's a true story, and what a favor he did her by telling her this brutal truth, one that very few dare to share. It's not the nicest comeback my friend had hoped for, to say the least, but it was necessary for her to have this painful experience when she already felt conflicted about her rates so she could begin to understand the psychology of pricing and its many paradoxes.

Low prices hurt you. Low prices are like cancer to a business. They grow, they cause pain and frustration for the business owners, and, if gone unchecked, they eventually kill the business. Low prices are not the way to the type of profitable, sustainable, long-term business that we seek as professionals.

You Alone are in Charge of Your Prices

My mastermind group peers and I had the very same problem with low prices, but we needed proof, so we did an experiment: we decided to raise our prices to the level that matched the perceived (and proven) value of our work and, boom, we started selling a lot faster. We did "The Money Game," designed by Rich Litvin, which asks you to focus on what you most control, which is the number of proposals you make rather than what you least control, the conversions from prospects to customers. Yes, you can influence the latter, but you 100% control the former, and it emphasizes the point again: you alone are in charge of your prices.

So, we got to work. We made outrageous proposals by following three simple rules:

1. We felt highly confident about our ability to help each individual with their particular challenge.
2. We came from a place of service, not selling or neediness or ego.
3. We were not allowed to assume, guess, or judge who can pay what, because we would be wrong 100% of the time. That is their business, not ours.

In the early part of this experiment, I proposed a number of $5,000 packages, which yielded a 20% conversion, but I noticed that the process was long and arduous, and I had to work really hard to position their value. I then started to propose packages at $15,000, $25,000, $30,000, $40,000, and $70,000, which to my shock yielded a 57% conversion, with far less effort and energy on my end. These new packages included longer contracts and a higher level of engagement, but the conversion rates were very encouraging, and the investments up front scaled well with my time and energy. As a result, I ended up delivering at a far higher value for fewer clients. In hindsight, if all my $5,000 proposals had come through, I'd have been booked with too many clients and too many small packages, and too busy to pursue higher proposals. This proposal taught me about scaling my time, energy and resources as I reached for my revenue goals, but that was just the beginning.

The experiment continued to surprise and delight me. The clients who invested at a much higher level treated the coaching as central to their business or career. They capitalized on everything they received. Their minds were open to new ideas and necessary shifts, and they were ready to take action when those shifts occurred. Naturally, their results matched their level of commitment.

Moreover, I noticed the positive changes in myself as a coach when I worked with higher-paying clients. I raised my own level of commitment, devotion to client success, and service, and I grew more as a coach than if I had taken on the easier problems, which would have kept me in my comfort zone. The success of the client was always important, but now I began to see my clients as an extension of myself, and while I was not *responsible* for their success—an important distinction in the coaching realm—I did everything to make sure *they* felt responsible for their own success. I found I cared deeply about these clients, not because they were paying me more, but because they were so committed to their own journeys. After all, it is always a privilege when an individual invites you along on their journey of transformation.

Most people who invest in coaching get the concept at a surface level and reap the benefits at the same level. My high-paying clients were going well below the surface. They were exploiting possibility upon possibility for themselves. They were discarding old identities that no longer served them. They were going deep. They didn't want 10% or 15% growth in their business; they were taking leaps. They refused to let their past experiences play a role in their future, and as I worked with them, I was able to witness something extraordinary.

Just as wasted potential is a depressing sight, realized potential is light and glory itself, especially that of someone you helped enable. This is not accidental. When you invest in yourself at uncomfortable levels, you tap into something magical. You know you have to make it work. You know you couldn't live with yourself if you wasted your investment. Too much is at stake even to consider failure as an option. So, you make the "impossible" happen because your mind believes that you can. And thus, you go beyond your edge.

You best realize your potential to serve others by charging appropriately for your services.

You are allowed to completely ignore your competitors' prices or the market as a whole—if you want to price yourself above all of that, the only justification you must have is to be able to first articulate the value of your offerings to yourself. If you are 100% convinced that what you have to offer is appropriate for what you intend to charge, you shall find buyers.

Bucking the trend, so to speak, happens every day in every industry and market. Take the $10,000 "designer" plastic handbags. They have proven the extremes possible on a pricing scale. When the designer of that first handbag got this idea in his or her head, knowing well that the average plastic handbag sold for $175, they went for outrageous and, at the time, impossible. While we can be certain that the ROI of $10,000 is *not* there for any designer plastic handbag, we can see that they sell.

Why? Because people love to pay premium prices. It makes them feel good. Emotions call the shots on these types of purchases, not logic. When you're buying oranges at Whole Foods and you know you could get them cheaper at Walmart, you are using logic in order to save $3.50. When you buy an expensive handbag for your wife's fiftieth birthday, you are not using logic, because the logic is laughable here. You are using your emotions and you are convinced it will be worth it.

I use this example not to suggest designer plastic handbags as a guide to follow for our professional services. Far from it—I use it to remind you that if you want to charge higher prices, you absolutely can. The only person standing in the way of making that happen is you. The only person whose permission you need is you.

Think about it: Do you have a product or service that can deliver far more ROI than a plastic handbag? Can you see yourself charging $10,000 or more for it? Can you envision yourself describing to a prospect the value of this investment? And can you feel good about it all?

Your Pricing Reflects Your Self-Worth

Pricing our services pushes the self-worth button. It doesn't matter if you are a solopreneur working from home or the president of an established firm with many employees; in my work with clients from all walks of life, pricing triggers a very vulnerable button: our self-worth.

My clients would argue with me, using their logic and rationale to mask the real issues. They would explain how they couldn't possibly raise prices, based on data and market value and competitors and so on and so forth. They have proof, too, because when they tried to raise them once, it backfired and nobody was buying. If you want to believe a myth, you will always be able to back it up with enough data to prove your point, and then the myth becomes your reality. But if you want to create a new reality, let go of the myth so you create space for this new reality.

We all know at least one entrepreneur who has found a way to charge precisely what he or she desires and has happy clients. How did they do it against all the odds that you are facing in the same market?

The odds are in your head, but not in theirs. So, you stop yourself while they enable themselves.

If you are less than 100% satisfied with what you are charging today, you are charging too little. There is a reason behind your dissatisfaction and, if left unexplored, it will grow over time into an annoying resentment. I've experienced it. My coach and consultant peers have experienced it. The resentment falls like a shadow on your creative genius and affects the deep quality of your work.

How do you know if this is happening? Pause and reflect. Ask yourself if you are thrilled with your prices in exchange for what you are delivering. If you said yes right away, skip to the next chapter. If you paused or said no or maybe, keep reading.

What often gets in the way is confusion about what low prices actually mean. We hurt ourselves by implying we are not as good as someone charging twice or three times as much, which is a reflection of our self-worth. We think too small. Why? Because small is familiar. Small is comfortable.

Just listen to aspiring business owners—while you have your ambitious types who are out to dominate the world (Apple, Amazon, Google), most business owners at the start of their journey cling to the myths below:

- They talk about their size (a reference to both company size and revenue): "Oh, I'm just going to open a small chiropractor practice, nothing fancy."
- They use the struggle mentality to justify low prices: "I'm doing some coaching work on the side. It's hard to get clients to pay, so I'm making it really affordable to work with me."
- They convince themselves their low revenue is just the way it is, not a direct outcome of their own doing: "I have my own consulting business. The pay is okay. Not as good as my old job, but it beats having a boss."
- They confuse business with charity because of the "money is evil" mindset at the base of their belief: "I'm happy if I can just stay in business. I'm not here to make a fortune or anything. My work is spiritual and for the greater good."

To this group, the ambitious, confident business owner comes across as egotistical, arrogant, even aggressive or overly confident, and can pose a threat to them, whereas the struggling, "humble," and "modest" entrepreneur is ideal to commiserate with.

Does any of this sound familiar to you? Do you or someone you know use this language when they talk about their business?

Your pricing reflects your self-worth, the amount you perceive you are worth in exchange for your goods and services. If your sense of self-worth is low, you are most likely underpricing yourself. You may feel guilty charging more. You relate to and have grown comfortable with the constant struggle of running a barely profitable business. You probably envy or resent your counterparts for their higher prices, and you see yourself as separate from them. You cannot see that you are where you are not because of any circumstance or outside decision made on your behalf; you are *exactly* where you put yourself.

The good news is that you can move. If you put yourself there, you can just as well get yourself out and move up the ladder of pricing. You are not separate from success, because success does not discriminate. You are connected to the same frequency of success that your counterparts are enjoying, but you can't stand in the way, complain, and expect miracles at the same time. You have to learn to get out of your own way. Let's see how we can help you do that and bring your self-worth and your pricing to match your incredible gifts and talents.

LIMITING BELIEF ONE: "IF I CAN'T MAKE A SMALL SALE, HOW CAN I POSSIBLY MAKE A BIG ONE? OBVIOUSLY, I'M ALREADY TOO EXPENSIVE."

Counterintuitive as it may be, people are more than willing to pay for "expensive" as long as they want what you have, they're not being sold, and they see the value. You will experience this as you move into higher echelons of service offerings and feel comfortable charging higher prices, but to get you there, we have to get you out of your limiting beliefs first.

When You Are Starting Out

My brother, Sina Bahram, runs Prime Access Consulting in Research Triangle Park, NC, which primarily helps organizations in the cultural heritage sector (such as galleries, libraries, archives, and museums) to implement universal designs in service and products offerings. His goal is to enable all of his clients to reach the widest audience possible.

Sina happens to be one of the *best* in the world in his industry, and the awards for and praise of his work (such as being recognized a White House Champion of Change by President Barack Obama for his work enabling users with disabilities to succeed in Science, Technology, Engineering, and Math (STEM) fields, as well as an Emerging Leader in Digital Accessibility Award at the annual Knowability Community Heroes of Accessibility Awards, among other accolades) have established him firmly in a well-respected spot in his market.

Sina admits that he never experienced any inner conflict about selling his services. At the beginning, he charged lower prices until he built up his portfolio and, along with it, his reputation, and he says this is key in building up one's confidence inertia: "It's really easy to keep a moving train going, but getting it started takes a ton of energy."

I asked Sina what advice he would give an equally smart and driven fellow entrepreneur who does not have confidence when starting out. His suggestion is to build up your confidence by direct experience and by continuing to iterate and failing forward again and again.

"Do the maximum amount of work upfront. In the first six to twelve months of your business, take *all the jobs* and don't worry about what you're getting paid. In fact, take the lower paying jobs. Screw them up if you must. Make all of your mistakes early on so that you don't mess up the $25,000, $50,000 or $500,000 contracts."

That's right—Sina goes so far as to advise you to say yes to all jobs at the beginning. He attributes the successes he's most benefited from in his life to his being unwilling to say no to opportunities. It's tempting to point to the negatives of this habit, such as higher stress and loss of personal boundaries, yet the opportunities have almost single-handedly dictated his entire career.

Case in point: He said yes to a fellow award recipient at the White House who invited him to join a workshop on museum accessibility the following week. Next thing he knows, he is one of the most-consulted experts in the world when it comes to museum accessibility. This is all due to being less discriminating and more eager for any opportunity early on in his business.

Now, as you grow with experience, you raise your prices, and you will have higher standards, so you can decline less lucrative offers and be selective with your clients as your reputation begins to establish itself.

"Selling to me is effortless," Sina says, "but what's important is that at the end of the relationship, my clients are DELIGHTED. If they're not delighted, I'm not happy. The money doesn't do it for me. It's great, but the stuff that really matters is when my clients are delighted at what we've accomplished."

The source of that delight is the transformation that happens to Sina's clients' mindsets. The clients start off thinking how painfully difficult and expensive it would be to build smart accessibility and design into their products, but after the experience, they see that not only is their initial perception false, there are also tons of benefits to what they accomplished by doing this work. They turn into evangelists of accessibility and rave to others about it. What better organic marketing could you wish for?

When You Reach the Level of a Pro

Let's imagine the beginning stages are behind you. The business has had its fifth anniversary. You are now a pro, a real professional, at what you do. You have a track record of success with clients and customers who love what you have.

How do you feel about your pricing now? Are you happy about what you charge? Are your customers glad to pay their invoices on time for the massive value they get from your work? Are you delighting these customers at the end of the day? Are you selective with your clients and choosing to work exclusively with other true professionals? As you reach the level of pro, all of this begins to falls into place.

As a pro, your prices are not a function of the market's going rate or your hunch about what your customer is willing to pay. Your prices are a direct correlation between what you intend to charge and what value you see in your offer. As a pro, you know this, because you don't see yourself as a commodity; you know there is only one of you. This is true whether you are a professional painter, a housing contractor, an IT consultant, a book editor, or any other profession in this book; as a pro, you know your worth and you charge accordingly. What's more, you feel good about it, and your customers feel good about it, too. You are not concerned with rejection, because you accept that you're not right for everyone. And because you feel reassured about your value, you are poised for success.

Why? Because this state of operation releases your creative genius, which constantly builds upon what you create. Any other state where you or your customers are not happy about your prices puts you in a stressful or anxious place, and that is poison for your creativity and performance. The state of worry, insecurity, inner conflict, or doubt sabotages you in all areas of life, often without your knowledge, and it is a downward spiral to increased levels of anxiety and decreased levels of success. This is what causes business owners to propagate the false-yet-popular notion that "Running a business is oh-so-hard!"

Is that really true? Not for a pro. Running a business is a joy if you stay aligned to your creative genius while generating massive value and revenue. It starts with the intention to create what matters to you and a decision to make it happen.

Example: A few years ago, my prices were nowhere near the value I delivered in my coaching, and with every client, I could see that I had underpriced myself yet again. I was an amateur not only because of the underpricing, but because I did not *see* how to get out of it, so instead, I grew resentful and lost the joy in my work. In fact, for a while there, I almost stopped coaching. The work to turn myself into a pro has been an intentional multi-year process (and is still ongoing).

In the end, I just went for it. I made large investments in my development. I learned how to position my value, how to have powerful conversations, how to really serve, how to establish a smart pricing model, how to create trust and build relationships, and how to consistently create ideal clients. Today, I am delighted with all my clients, and they are delighted with what they are creating. When all of these components fall into place, we create unexpected results.

Experiment to Create a New Reality

Experimenting helped me break out of the limiting mindset we're discussing in this section: If I couldn't sell those smaller packages, how could I possibly sell the bigger ones? Experimenting answered that.

I did not believe anything until I could actually do it. I needed a new reality to reference. I just couldn't believe that a prospect who is hesitant about a $375 package would be willing to pay $3,750, and to do so with more delight and far less effort on my part. To my shock, it turns out that is *exactly* the case, and you can do the math on selling ten of the former package with sweat or ten of the latter packages with ease. Life was suddenly very different for me as a coach.

The first step, then, is to experiment: Triple your rates on the next conversation with a prospect tomorrow. Quadruple it for the next one. Experiment. If the new rates scare you to death, you're on the right track. Your limiting belief is probably so strong that it wants to stop you, but resist it. You are just experimenting.

Can you give yourself permission to play with your pricing? Of course you can. You are your own boss, remember. And I'll give you a great reason: After you do this just once, after you book a single client at ten times your current rate, you won't go back. It's done. It's the point of no return on your journey to turning pro. So your experiment here is to make the leap, to do the unthinkable and book one client at your new rate, and to let that be your new norm. And yes, it IS that simple and that possible.

So why is it easier to sell premium packages with ease? How does this paradox work?

It's in the perception. You are perceived as a "cheap" brand if your prices are low or mediocre, no matter how brilliant you are at your craft. Cheap brands attract a certain caliber of customers and clients, and from first-hand experiences of myself and people I respect, we find that this caliber is often more demanding, less appreciative and much more challenging to work with. As you can see, the paradox continues.

As you move into the upper echelons, though, you are attracting a new caliber of customers and clients. They get this pro level because they normally hire pros. They are used to paying premium prices for high quality. They are professionals themselves and will treat you with respect and appreciate your work even as they pay more for it.

To be able to attract, secure, and serve such a caliber of clients and customers, you must first see yourself as worthy, and to do so, you must—absolutely positively MUST—be very good at what you do. This is non-negotiable. Are *you* really good at what you do? Can you speak to a track record of success? Can you see the real value of what you are delivering and confidently speak to it? Can you be unattached to closing every deal and making every sale? Then you are ready to command your ideal prices, and you're on your way to turning pro.

LIMITING BELIEF TWO: "PEOPLE WON'T PAY FOR THE HIGHER PRICE, BECAUSE THEY CAN GET IT CHEAPER ELSEWHERE."

You know from your life experience that cheap comes with a price, and often a higher price than we bargain for.

So yes, some people will be looking for the absolute lowest price in the product or service. Some people will always be price shopping, but guess what? You can run a profitable and sustainable business and *never* sign a single person who is price shopping. You have that prerogative.

I remember that when I was much younger, even though I made really good money at my corporate job, I had a scarcity mindset so bad that price alone drove *all* my decisions. "How much is it?" was my ubiquitous response to everything. If this plumber was cheaper, I'd bring him in. If that painter was cheaper, she was hired. If this car-service place was the cheapest, I'd never go anywhere else. Paying for a premium service was not on my radar.

If the old me is the kind of customer you want, that's one approach to your business, but not the one I'm teaching you here. If you are establishing a premium brand, a high-quality product, or a top-of-the-line service, you can skip right over the price shopper and take comfort in the fact that cheap customers can never be the foundation of the kind of business a pro like you plans to run. I would never want the "old me" as a client!

"If you think it's expensive to hire a professional to do the job, wait until you hire an amateur."
—Unknown

Now that you have skipped over the segment of the market shopping for the lowest price, you can move to the next-level segment: they want a good deal and they are willing to pay for high-quality service. You have now positioned yourself in the more selective segment of the market. This segment cares about all things high-quality, professional, and premium. They care nothing about paying bottom dollar; in fact, they feel good about paying high prices. The product can be anything: IT service, luggage, a T-shirt, vitamin supplements, yoga lessons, life coaching, you name it; they will only buy from someone who cares about them and who really understands them.

Confession: I happen to be a bit of a savvy consumer these days. Years of shopping brands online or around the world and doing hundreds of reviews of products have equipped me well with stories. My favorite is about the Patagonia luggage we bought for our first trip to Japan in 2004.

It was made of hard nylon, the kind from which parachutes are made. My husband was gentle and kind with his, but I crammed an unreasonable volume into mine on our trips around the globe. One day, the fabric lining the zipper of the top compartment tore. I was crushed. I called

Patagonia and complained that my eight-year-old luggage was no longer usable. They offered to have me ship it back for free repair. Free. Repair.

I had my repaired good-as-new luggage back in two weeks. Several trips later and my packing habit still unchanged, I tore it again, and this time a lot worse. Another phone call and we shipped it back to Patagonia at their suggestion. A week later, they sent back an apology letter. They had decided the luggage was beyond repair, and so they refunded me a large portion of what I paid for it in the form of a gift card to spend however I wished in their store.

Result: Customer Delight for Life.

I do not shop Patagonia regularly today, yet if I wanted something specific, I *wouldn't hesitate* to buy from them, even if it's double the price of their competitors. I rave about Patagonia. I'm a fan for life. This brand has shown me the value of customer care through acts of generosity beyond reason.

Another example is my shopping experience at my favorite yoga clothing online store, Liquido Active. I had shopped their online store a few times and thought I knew my size. But when I got my latest sports bra, it was too big, and I'd already taken off all the tags. So I emailed the lovely folks at Liquido Active.

They asked me a few questions and then they sent me a gift card equivalent to the original price of the bra, even though I had bought it at a discount, and asked me to keep the bra anyway. I'm not switching to another line of yoga clothing anytime soon. Liquido Active clothes sell at about two times the price of other yoga apparel. I gladly pay the difference without thinking twice about it. What I hope for you to see with these stories is the impact of deep caring and the unexpected consequences it can achieve in terms of building trust, earning loyalty and even raving fans for you. It is a simple action with massive results, and it is the demonstration of true service that we have been talking about all along.

Your Business Prices are a Direct Reflection of Your Personal Values

Our businesses are an extension of ourselves. What you value in your life will reflect in your business. For instance, if you are a bargain shopper everywhere in your personal life, you may have a real challenge with pricing yourself, say, in the top 1% of your market. Your subconscious would argue that's anything but attractive to the bargain shopper. Even if you see your business as separate from your personal life, you are the common denominator in both. This is where conflicts of values arise: you are a bargain shopper on one side and an aspiring premium-service provider on the other, and therein lies the dilemma.

If you're constantly chasing bargain deals at home and then attempting to do the opposite in your business, you will feel disoriented jumping from one personality to another. Take a closer look at what makes you a bargain shopper and the beliefs behind this behavior that make it worth your time and energy. There are naturally different levels of bargain shopping, from a fun hobby to a strict mode of operating. If you are the latter, dig deeper. Until you resolve your views on bargain shopping, you cannot comfortably and confidently raise prices in your business to ambitious levels.

If bargain shopping is a core value in your life, you may resonate with the false belief that nobody will pay a higher price if they can get it lower elsewhere. If you live and breathe this value, you will see everyone as being on the same frequency as yourself. The people you attract into your business then will naturally be sharing the bargain-shopping mentality, so you will box yourself into a price zone that satisfies them. These are your customers, you argue, and they won't "let" you command higher prices. As you protect the bargain shopper, you push away the high-paying premium customer.

If you want to command higher prices in your business, you have to break out of constantly chasing bargains in your personal life first. You have to be able to appreciate paying premium prices for premium service.

You have to create that experience in your own body first before you ask others to do the same.

In other words, you have to walk your talk.

Walk Your Talk

This brings me to one of my pet peeves. In the coaching world, for instance, the coaches who struggle the most with getting clients are those who have trouble walking their own talk. They want to coach you to have more success and happiness in your life, your career, your business, and yet they have never hired their own coaches. They want you to pay them thousands of dollars, but they have yet to bring themselves to do the same. If the roles were reversed, they would *neither* take their own advice *nor* pay their own fees. Because they have not yet overcome their limiting beliefs about investing in their own growth and development, they have a hard time convincing anyone else to do the same, and that's precisely why they stay a struggling coach.

Compare that to what happens when you walk your talk. That's what I attribute for going from struggling to thriving coach, from amateur to pro. In my ongoing coaching education, I have so far invested upwards of $65,000 in my private coaches, programs, and masterminds, and gladly continue to do so, and I happen to be on the low end of the spectrum as compared to my ultimate role models. The education of a pro coach never ends, and it is this insatiable curiosity, combined with the willingness to live out one's own principles, that empowers a coach to charge appropriately for his or her services.

Without walking my talk, it would have been impossible for me to accumulate the three pillars: the confidence and the expertise and the mindset to reach this level of success. My own personal values had to shift FIRST before my business began to reflect a similar shift. Your business and personal life are very much connected, so if you want to break this or similar limiting beliefs, put your own house in order first.

Why People Pay More for a Service or Product

The false assumption behind this limiting belief, that people won't pay for the higher price because they can get it cheaper elsewhere, is that they are getting the *exact same experience in both places*. If one could get the same exact experience for a low, medium, or high price, who in their right mind would pay the high price?

But it is not the same experience.

A premium product or service creates a different experience with a higher value. Like what, you wonder? Let's take service first: A professional service comes with years of experience, during which the professional has made tons of mistakes, learned from them, and grown into an expert who knows how to do his craft better than his peers. An amateur service lacks experiences and expertise, and what you "save" in dollars (or other currencies) when you pay for the lower price, you make up for it in lower quality of work, in mistakes and rework, in less professionalism, and other frustrations such as lack of timeliness, reliability, and trust, all of which taint the overall experience. You may save money, but you're not getting the same experience.

Sometimes, you do get great service for cheap, but it is more often the exception than the rule. The customer who is willing to pay more knows this and wants certainty—inasmuch as one can have it in this world—of having the best experience. This type of customer values her own time and energy and wants to work with a pro, not an amateur. The pro gets the message and knows how to cater to her.

So, again, why would someone pay more for a service or product? In short, to be able to create the kind of experience that matters most to them and aligns best to their values. The product or service is not just a means to an end for this savvy consumer. It is a process by which they create an experience. The end result matters, yes, but not as much as the process that gets you there. The pro understands this and that's their secret to delivering above and beyond every time.

If you want to serve this type of customer, you need to set yourself up in a way that appeals and speaks to her directly.

Effortless Selling, Premium Prices, and the Joys of True Service

The real joy of service comes when you realize that not only can you create customers and clients for your premium prices, and not only are you able to rise to that level of service or product delivery, but that it is far more effortless to sell higher packages and more premium services than it is to sell the low-end versions.

This is counterintuitive at first, but after you practice it, you will find it to be true in practice, provided that you nod yes to the following seven conditions:

1. You are 100% clear on the value you deliver.
2. You believe completely in what you do and why you do it.
3. You are able to articulate this value well in the language of your prospective buyers.
4. You are able to address potential objections to your price.
5. You are unattached from closing and converting every prospect, and only focused on serving.
6. You have zero doubts about your ability to deliver and your worthiness to get paid at this level.
7. You only offer this service to those who are a perfect match for what you need (unless, as Sina mentioned in the previous section, you are in the very early stages of your business and may need to be less selective until you get established).

Are you operating at this level in your business, or do you see gaps that need to be closed first? The conditions above prepare you for effortless selling, and you need to feel confident that every single one is firmly in place. When everything above is in place, the selling happens organically. It is a natural outcome from the culmination of all that you bring to the table.

When my yoga teacher is helping me with an impossibly difficult yoga pose, her perspective is this: "It is not about *getting* it. It is about *allowing* it to happen by doing everything else I've taught you." This applies to selling, too.

Effortless selling then isn't a goal for which to aim; the goal is to serve. Selling is an organic outcome of having all the right foundations in place. When you create your foundation, selling premium-priced services becomes effortless. The struggle to sell goes away. The joy of service takes its place. The outcomes emerge without you having to force them. Keep this in mind as you do the work and trust the process all the way there.

LIMITING BELIEF THREE: "WHO AM I TO CHARGE HIGH PRICES? I FEEL GUILTY ABOUT CHARGING A LOT. I FEEL SHAME AROUND RECEIVING MONEY."

Remember how we talked about our mindset taking shape over the course of our life? Part of that mindset, as it relates to our work here, is our beliefs around money. Our conditioning around money starts forming at a very young age. Our upbringing, our families and other important people in our life play a key role in those formative years in influencing how we think and feel about money.

For example, if you grew up in a struggling household where money was always tight, and where it was tough to make ends meet, you likely still carry those ideas around with you. In fact, even if you are now prosperous by all measures, there is a non-zero chance you are still harboring some limitations around money from your earlier conditioning, and often without your knowledge. I've seen the surprise on my clients' faces when they've reassured me that they are totally fine around money until I challenge them to elevate their financial goals beyond their comfort zone, or increase the stakes on a negotiation, or set up a higher pricing strategy. They look like they've hit a wall.

Before learning this new mindset, that wall felt real and impenetrable to me. Even though I really wanted to raise my prices, I couldn't bring myself to do it. I'd raise them by 10% and then be fraught with doubt and insecurity that nobody would pay them. I'd second-guess my ability to deliver the value. A part of me really wanted to operate at a higher level, but my subconscious held me captive to this limiting belief that I was not worthy of "high prices." My brain may not have used those exact words, but the message came through loud and clear: "Who are you to charge those prices?," "Who would even pay them?," or "What can you give them to make it worth that much?"

The first time I raised my hourly rate from $80 to $95, I was shocked that the prospect agreed to the new rate without objecting. I was anticipating a rejection so much that I went speechless for a few seconds. It turns out she did not echo the doubts in my head. The doubts in my head were *only* in my head. That's when I wanted to know: Where do the doubts come from? How can I send them back and be rid of them for good?

Guilt, Shame, and Knowing the Difference

The two most common emotions around a scarcity mindset are guilt and shame. You may have heard them used interchangeably, but guilt and shame are two distinct emotions.

Shame is an identity or a label we give ourselves anytime we use statements of a fixed identity such as "I am" or "I am not." With shame, we perceive the issue to be fixed and unchangeable. Best-selling author Dr. Brené Brown has devoted her research to helping people overcome shame, which, according to Brown, "corrodes the very part of us that believes we are capable of change."

Guilt, on the other hand, is how we feel about a behavior, a decision, or an action, such as something we did or didn't do that may have had negative consequences.

Shame is a gaping emotion that implies we are deeply flawed, whereas guilt points to a mistake, a faux-pas about which we feel terrible. Guilt can be a motivator for change, and we generally talk about it openly, whereas shame is deep-rooted and heavy, so we hide it and don't talk about it. Shame labels you, whereas guilt speaks to an annoying action or a frustrating decision.

Can you begin to tell the difference between guilt and shame yet? It's important to distinguish between the two so you know right away which one is coming up for you and how to overcome the right obstacle.

Let's give it some context. Say you miss a meeting. If your inner voice says: "I am such a loser; I do this all the time," that's shame. If your inner voice says, "Today I kinda messed up," that's guilt. Or, say you committed to a phone call with a client, and completely forgot about it. If your inner voice says, "I'm hopeless. I never remember my commitments. I always do this," that's shame. If your inner voice says, "Oh no! I forgot about the call! How embarrassing! I'd better make up for it to the client," that's guilt.

As you learn the distinction between guilt and shame, observe which one you most experience when it comes to setting your pricing, charging appropriately for your services, or, even further yet, receiving the appropriate fees that you set for yourself.

What is at the Root of Shame?

In the words of one of our contemporary scholars of shame, Gershen Kaufman, "Shame is the most disturbing experience individuals ever have about themselves; no other emotion feels more deeply disturbing, because in the moment of shame, the self feels wounded from within." As you can see, shame is a powerful force that can derail our best intentions, but as we learn more about it, we can come out as the stronger force.

At the root of your shame, you always find a perceived undesirable identity which you want to avoid at all costs. For instance, the identity would be in the blank if you say to yourself, "Oh! I don't want people to think I am ____" where the blank could be successful, smart, rich, wealthy, comfortable, etc. In other words, shame says I don't want to be different because different doesn't belong.

Shame wants you to feel and think and believe that wealth comes with a price (no pun intended) and that price is being different and therefore separate from your tribe as they know you. Your friends and family, for instance, know you to be a relatively successful entrepreneur, even if you work really hard and struggle on occasion. What would happen if you suddenly stopped struggling, if you felt happy and confident, if you had no more stories of "business is slow this month!" and if you cut down your hours and started traveling first class to exotic locations? Would you experience a sense of separation or of closeness to your tribe as a result of these new levels of prosperity? Most people believe they would experience separation or a "casting out" from the tribe, and in this case, being an outcast is the undesirable identity.

So even though say a higher profit in business can lead to a better life, the shameful part of you is unwilling to pay the price at the risk of being cast out. Thus, you resist prosperity and you sabotage your own efforts towards it. You prefer the familiar to the unknown, i.e., belonging with your tribe to being cast out, and in this way, shame "protects" you against the so-called undesirable identity—or it feels as if it does, at least.

As Dr. Jane Bolton, a psychotherapist and coach, said in *Psychology Today* on what we get wrong about shame: "When I talk about shame, I'm not talking about anyone actually DOING anything wrong. I'm talking about the FEELING and the thoughts that we are somehow wrong, defective, inadequate, not good enough, or not strong enough."

Even though the undesirable identity is a positive outcome—successful business owner, prosperous entrepreneur, flourishing start-up founder—you will resist it because it may trigger a sense of separation, jealousy, or resentment from your tribe, especially if most of your tribe members are struggling in the very areas in which you are now excelling. Shame will hold you bound to your tribe and thus block your eventual prosperity. As long as the undesirable identity is taking up space in your subconscious, you will be operating below your glorious peak and without reaching your authentic possibilities, and this is why shame is too expensive a price to pay.

While guilt may play a role in undercharging in your business, it is shame that drives the thoughts that claim your situation to be hopeless or make you think "this is just the way I am." If you can address the shame, the guilt usually follows suit and you will have cleared the path of both obstacles.

Now, there are times that you may consciously choose to contribute to a cause or a mission or forgo your rates on purpose for a certain customer. That is your prerogative. Professional speakers speak for free at causes that are important to them. Businesses engage in charities all the time. Coaches do free coaching at special events or conferences. Business owners offer their services at no charge as they see fit, but the reason they can afford to do this is because they have already established a successful enterprise through a smart pricing model: They are clear on their worth. They are confident about their fees. Intention, rather than shame or guilt, drives their decisions on how to best use their limited time and energy toward their larger vision. So you can price yourself free or low with intention and clarity as you see fit, but if you are doing it because you feel you have "no other choice," that is shame talking. Here are four steps you can take to rise above guilt and shame when it comes to charging appropriately and happily receiving that which you are asking in exchange for your goods and services:

Step One: Become Aware of the Self-Talk

Let's say you've set a new price. Pay attention to the inner chatter in your head and tap into any guilt or shame talk there. How do you REALLY feel when you say your new prices out loud to a prospect? What does the voice in your head say about this new price?

If you have a hard time hearing your inner voice at first, let's try something else. Have a seat with a straight spine, get quiet and calm, close your eyes, and see if you notice a shift in your energy as you say your new price. See if you feel any discomfort or "butterflies in your stomach" or any muscles tightening as you think about raising the bar on the investment level for working with you. Many times, when we feel imbalanced about money, we feel it first in our body, and becoming aware of that is the first step toward positive change.

Step Two: Catch It and Interrupt It

Now if you were able to hear your inner voice, great. Next, you need to go into an observation mode where you listen to your self-talk and discern whether you are doing the guilt talk or the shame talk.

As you hear the shame or guilt talk happening, your task is to catch yourself and interrupt the process, as we did earlier where we rewrote the script of your narrative. To make the interruption most effective, when you hear yourself say, "I'm hopeless with money," an I AM statement that falls under the shame category, actually pause what you're doing. Catch yourself in the act and interrupt yourself. Speak out loud to make it real. You might say: "OK, I'm doing it again, but I'm stopping now because it's not true!" The more you do this, the easier it becomes and the earlier you catch yourself in the process.

Other examples of shame talks around money are:

- I am arrogant if I charge higher prices.
- I am selfish and self-centered if I want more income.
- I am conceited with a big fat ego if I want to be wealthy.
- I am flaky or irresponsible with money.
- I am hopeless with my finances.
- I am bad at being in business for myself.

If, on the other hand, you hear yourself ask, "Who can afford to pay these higher prices?" or "Would it be fair of me to charge this rate?" you are feeling guilt before taking an action such as raising your prices. Other examples of guilt talk about money may be:

- I feel terrible charging more than my peers.
- Higher prices means my current customers won't afford me.
- Higher prices means cheaper customers can't afford me.
- I may offend people with my higher prices.
- I may alienate my business peers.

If you can't hear your self-talk at all, but can still feel an imbalance of energy in your body like we mentioned before, read the shame and guilt statements above out loud and see whether they resonate with you. For instance, read out loud: "I am arrogant if I charge higher prices. Is that true for me?" or "I feel terrible charging more than my peers. Is that true for me?"

If you feel you can relate to that statement, it's likely true for you. Doing this should help you get some clarity as to whether you lean more toward guilt or shame.

As you observe your harsh self-talk and work to catch it, incorporate in your inner voice those earlier elements with which we were gracing our prospects: curiosity, empathy, and kindness. Instead of berating yourself that you feel "arrogant for charging higher prices," use a loving voice to talk back. Maybe you would gently say to yourself, "OK, I am charging higher prices, but I wonder if that really makes me arrogant? Could I charge higher prices and be compassionate and caring at the same time?"

Talk back to yourself as if you are your own best friend analyzing a situation. Notice that your energy will begin to shift when you participate in the conversation with kindness and lack of judgment. As we noted earlier, the Dalai Lama says, "Love is the absence of judgment." Can you offer that kind of love to yourself here?

Step Three: Share It If It's Shame

Let's set the guilt talk aside for now. If you found that the root of your self-talk is shame, it's time to share it. As we said earlier, we hide our shame. We are, pun (finally!) intended, deeply ashamed of this shame. And the way your shame survives is in the dark, safe secrecy deep inside you. How do you make shame disappear? You expose it to light. You do that by sharing your shame.

Who can you trust to share this shame with? Who in your life would listen to you without judging you? Share your shame with them. Choosing the right person here is paramount.

If your shame is about your monthly income being in dire straits as a result of your low prices and few clients, then your life partner may be too close to hear you out objectively; they may share the money concerns, and while that is a valid topic, you don't want to combine discussing the problem with the shame-sharing. Your parents or siblings may be too worried about you, and maybe they were never onboard with this idea of "entrepreneurship" to begin with, so they too would not be the best people with whom to share your shame. Your best friend may want to make you feel better and fill you up with conciliatory platitudes, and while the intention comes from a good place, it misses the mark on what you need.

Instead, share your shame with an impartial friend, a coach, a mentor, a peer in the industry, or a mastermind buddy with whom you feel a deep trust and openness. Be very clear as to what you need from them in terms of support: what you need with shame sharing is to be heard with empathy and compassion and non-judgment. That's all. Your shame cannot survive the sharing, so when you shine a light on it by sharing it, you will have taken the first step to reclaim your power.

None of this is going to feel comfortable or easy at first, but everything is relative in life. Brené Brown puts it in a great perspective when she says, "I choose discomfort now over resentment later." The discomfort of overcoming your guilt and shame around money now is far easier than living with the eventual resentment of staying stuck where you are and watching opportunities for growth and prosperity pass you by!

LIMITING BELIEF FOUR: "I MIGHT OFFEND THEM WITH MY HIGH PRICES."

Sales is a conversation. You are exploring together to see if what you have to offer is indeed to the absolute benefit of the customer and they, in turn, are looking to see if your services are the right fit for them. This conversation is more like a creative process than a confrontation. The limiting belief says if you quote a very high price for your services, you may offend John or Jane if they cannot afford it. First of all, you don't know what they are willing to invest in order to solve this challenge in their life or achieve that result in their business, and none of this has anything to do with offending someone.

To inquire into this limiting belief, ask yourself: How and why would I offend them exactly? How do I disrespect someone by sharing the investment amount to hire me in exchange for my help? How am I overstepping my bounds in any way by sharing the arrangements of this exchange? Remember, by now, you have already asked permission to do this and they have agreed.

A Dummy's Guide to Offending Someone

I remember an incident many years ago when I was a young corporate employee back at Cisco. I had learned recently through an information leak that I was grossly underpaid in my peer group, even after getting the required top industry certification, so the issue of pay was particularly sensitive. That day, I was working with the executive administrator on a project in a conference room when one of the managers walked in. In the conversation that ensued, he talked about his recent vacation at a beach house. I got curious and asked where they had stayed. His response, before he could catch himself, was: "Oh! You can't afford that place!"

I froze in place. My cheeks grew hot. I was mortified, even if he had been the one doing the offending. The executive administrator immediately tried to soften the tension in the room. She turned to the manager and said, "Well, you don't know that! You don't know what she and her husband can afford." And he most certainly did not. My husband and I have always been fiscally conservative, and we could have afforded whatever we wanted even then.

Now *that* is how you most certainly offend someone. You assume. You judge. You make up a story about them. You say something stupid and make yourself look a total fool in the process.

The Big Paradox of Affordability

Never, EVER, EVER(!), assume to know what others are willing to pay for your services, because (A) It is none of your business, (B) You can't possibly know their full situation or their level of desire for what you offer, and (C) You unfairly limit your own business possibilities.

It is natural to want to put our prospects in boxes. This person can't afford me. This other person should easily pay my fees. That company won't pay that amount, but they'll pay this. We do this subconsciously, but it's about as accurate as throwing darts in the dark. This deeply ingrained habit leads to wrong assumptions and missed opportunities again and again and yet again.

In my conversations with now hundreds of prospects, I have never once correctly guessed who can pay what on either side of the spectrum. The judgment we pass on our prospects is unfair to them and us both, and *that* is the real offense, whether we make it up in our head or, worse, communicate it to the prospect.

Affordability is a misunderstood fear. It misinforms your mind about your next client. Your mind claims to know who can afford what. It knows no such thing. This subject does not concern you, so drop all such assumptions. Your only job is to serve, and to allow the serving to lead both parties to the best decision. Your job is to see if you are the right fit to help this person or business, not to run a mental accounting check on their finances from a severely limited view.

Logic and rationale are of little use here. I felt very resistant to this concept. I had to put my strong left brain on pause and see the big picture for what it really was. I wanted proof and proof showed up in the form of the right clients at just the right time.

My old logical thinking believed that big companies with enormous budgets would be more than willing to pay my executive coaching fees, and that corporate executives with large salaries and disposable income could easily afford my prices. That could not be further from the truth. Again and again, I found the most resistance securing clients in those areas, even when my fees were a fraction of today's. My highest-paying clients, who have faithfully stayed with me for years now, are small businesses with modest budgets, entrepreneurs at the earliest stages of the game where the risk is highest, corporate professionals in mid-level management who badly want to create a meaningful career and life for themselves, and extraordinary individuals with very ordinary incomes and very big dreams who decide to invest in the greatest asset of all: their own growth and development.

I could not have known about this paradox if I had not released my severe limiting beliefs around affordability and committed myself to totally serving the individual before me and allowing all else to emerge organically. I encourage you to drop all your assumptions about affordability. To determine who can afford what is simply unknowable to us.

Remember again, your only job is to serve. Your prospect's job is to decide if they want your help with their problem or that of someone else. What a liberation not to have to pass judgments on affordability on everyone who inquires about our services or to worry that you might offend them in the process.

GUIDING PRINCIPLE: INSIST ON A COMMITMENT THAT MATCHES THE INVESTMENT

A HIGHER INVESTMENT DEMANDS a higher commitment from your customers. When you ask for a higher investment to engage you on a project or to hire you on a contract, the stakes are higher for you. You are charging prices that only a pro would charge, and you are promising results that only a pro would promise. Your commitment to success is higher than ever before. And here's why that's crucial: This state of commitment brings out your absolute best; your brightest, your most creative, your most authentic, your most professional and caring self. My old college professor used to say that we do our absolute best under sufficient pressure. Well, the right high-paying client is the ideal kind of such pressure. It brings the best out of the pro!

But you're *not* the only one who benefits from the high stakes. Your client has made a large investment in working with you. Whether that investment was easy or hard for them to make, whether that is 0.0001% of their savings or 10% of it, it matters little after the contract is signed and the money transferred over. What matters is that they made an investment that went beyond their comfort zone. That discomfort works in their favor. Their very best version emerges through the discomfort.

How? Because they are now committed to getting the most out of their investment. They are inspired to take action and be active participants in the relationship, regardless of the nature of the business, and to capitalize on the investment they made.

So, know this: when you raise the bar for yourself and the kind of business you operate, you are demanding a higher level of commitment from your customers, too. In the end, you both win. This is the opposite of selfish. This is the integration of success and prosperity through a higher mutual commitment.

The stakes are higher when you charge appropriately for your services. And this level of discomfort is precisely what you and your clients need in order to reach new heights of success and fulfillment.

MINDSET FIVE: ADDRESS VOICED AND UNVOICED OBJECTIONS.

WE'VE BEEN TOTALLY PRESENT with our prospects. We've fully listened and adapted our style as necessary to best relate to and connect with them. We've earned their trust. We've asked permission before proposing an ideal solution that best serves them. Now we enter the most delicate part of the conversation: addressing any and all objections to our proposal.

Here's the definition of objection: an expression or feeling of disapproval or opposition; a reason for disagreeing.

In any business, you will come across objections in one form or another. Most business owners skirt around the issues, pretend they didn't hear or understand, and hope they'll quietly go away. But they won't.

The only way out is through—through the objections by addressing them head-on and overcoming them if possible, and doing so with full transparency and sincerity.

Stop Calling It Your "Baby"

It's natural to get invested in your creations on a deep level. It's normal to be beyond devoted and committed to your business and to see it as an extension of yourself. Passionate business owners live and breathe this.

But it's a terrible idea to call your business your baby and to attach so much sentiment and personal feeling to it. You hear phrases like:

- "My book is my baby."
- "My product is my baby."
- "My business is my baby."

But it's critical that you keep a healthy distance between you and your business, because your business isn't your baby. Your business will have problems and issues, for which it will require objectivity to see things as they are and take proper action. Rather than protecting your business from harm, something you would do unconditionally for your baby, you may have to shut your current business and start another one. You may have to exit through an acquisition. You may have to bring in a partner or declare bankruptcy. These critical decisions need an impartial leader at the helm.

Publishing my physical books taught me this lesson well. When my second book, *The Healthy Smoothie Bible*, would get a two-star Amazon review, I'd scroll past all the other five-star reviews to read what this "idiot" had to say about my "baby!" My ever-present instinct wanted to defend my work as I would my baby naturally. The criticism of a stranger on the book hit me so hard that it wiped out all the positive praise in its wake.

At the time, I misunderstood my role as an author. We are not here to "defend" our work. The best books in the world have one-star reviews. We are here to put our work out in the world and to let the world receive it as it will. We must exercise detachment to all reviews of our work—the good, the bad, and the ugly.

It's the ultimate exercise in vulnerability, letting go of what you can't control, and finding the joy in the impact you are having. A few weeks ago, my publisher called and asked us to write a third book in this series because the reviews are so strong and the book is in such high demand. Apparently, they could not care less about a few two-star reviews either, so again, why would I?

When you put your work out in the world, it will be praised and it will be criticized, and none of it will have *anything* to do with you. When you truly understand and internalize this truth, you will walk the path of a business owner with joy.

So stop calling it your baby. Establishing this distance between yourself and the outputs of your creative genius prepares you for the inevitable which awaits us all: the world of objections.

How well do you understand the word objection and how quickly do you spot it when your prospect has raised an objection concerning working with you?

For our purposes, an objection is a prospect's concerns or questions about an offer we have put forth. Let us learn to address them in a powerful way.

An Objection is Not a Rejection of You

Objections can cause a rainbow of negative emotions: awkwardness, shame, rejection, discomfort, disappointment, surprise, loss of direction or focus, and even humiliation. These emotions are messy and sometimes even heavy. It's no wonder that most of us would rather evade all objections, assume they don't exist, or hope they get magically resolved in the prospect's head, preferably without our intervention!

A business owner might go to great lengths to avoid perceived shame, humiliation, and all its ugly cousins. He may leave money on the table. She could walk out on a potentially big deal. He would tell himself a good story, like "they weren't going to buy anyway!" She would justify that it was already a lost cause, and move on to a "nicer, more pleasant client who really wants to work with me." All these misconceptions and assumptions form as a result of the false stories we weave, which paralyze us in the face of objections and for which, you may recall, we used the powerful tools of Byron Katie to inquire into the truth of our stories.

The false story makes it all about *you,* and that's the real blind spot. Objections are not about you. They are not a rejection of you. They are not a personal attack on your work. You are safe. Go ahead and take off the blinders.

Objections are your best allies in conversations and interactions with your prospects. You'll want objections. You'll invite objections. You'll welcome objections. You'll to see them as gifts for your business. In fact, you are going to *crave* objections when you're done learning this mindset.

The Obvious: Voiced Objections

There are two kinds of objections. The first one is a voiced objection: one where the prospect is voicing their objection and openly sharing what's on their mind. This is when your prospect comes back with a statement or a question regarding an outstanding offer or proposal. This can happen immediately when you present such an offer, or it can be a few days later. Here are some examples of voiced objections:

1. "We want to work with you, but it's outside our budget."
2. "Love to take you up on it, but I just can't afford it."
3. "I am all in, but I have to get my partner's approval."
4. "I've never hired someone. I'm a little uncomfortable doing it."
5. "The project timeline is longer than we had hoped."
6. "How do I know this solution will solve my problem?"
7. "I'll have to think about it. I'll get back to you."
8. "Could you give us a discount since we were referred to you?"

First, you need to learn how to process the objection in a way that helps you address it dispassionately. Imagine stepping to a higher perspective where you can observe what is happening between you and the prospect, so instead of being in the situation, you are now observing it, an outsider looking in. Can you now see it from your prospect's viewpoint?

Next, you have to put objections in context. They range from objection to price, to lack of trust that you're the right person, to ambiguity about the solution and its relevance to their specific problem, to deferring the decision to someone else. You need to address each objection according to its own context.

You do this by coming from that place of serving, curiosity, and empathy. You aim to educate and inform and help your prospect arrive at the right decision for *them*.

Then, you need to know exactly what to say, how to phrase it, what tone of voice to use, and how to navigate the rest of that dialogue to serve your prospect, all the while being detached from the goal of closing the deal.

Knowing what to say when you hear an objection is critical in helping take the right next step. One useful question that applies to just about any voiced objection is this: "I'm curious: What makes you say that?"

It's an open-ended question that invites the prospect to tell you more. Then comes the Golden Rule of all objections: Always—ALWAYS—ask follow-up questions before you even begin to respond. This is hard to do if you are in a hurry, if you feel you know the answer, or if you are uncomfortable and want to get things "over with," so calm yourself down. You must slow down here, pause, and learn more first. Remember: the rule of thumb is to always respond to the objection with an open-ended question first.

Because of social norms and speech etiquette, our prospects take care to phrase their initial objections in a politically correct way. In other words, they mask the real issue in a white lie. If they say they can't afford it, that can in fact be the real objection, but a *real* affordability issue is rare, as you will see. However, the facade of affordability often covers the actual objection. The phrases "outside my budget" or "I can't afford it" are often showstoppers, because most business owners don't know where to go from there. What you need to find out in these situations is what's behind this initial objection.

If you hear the "I can't afford it" objection, probe further by exploring any of the avenues below:

- What is their level of desire?
- What is their level of trust in you being the right person/company?

- What is their greatest fear about making this commitment?
- What is their biggest doubt about the solution?
- What are their competing priorities?
- What is their sense of urgency?

Most of my clients are often surprised to find out the real reason masked behind the "affordability" cover after I teach them to dig deeper with their prospects. It takes courage and clear communication and compassion to go there with your prospect. Don't let them off the hook after the infamous "I can't afford it" as long as you are unattached from closing the deal and stay in service to them.

Your prospect in turn appreciates this, even if they don't voice it. Very few in a business transaction show this level of care and curiosity after the prospect has essentially "turned down their offer," because they don't see the objection as the huge opportunity that it is. They see it as the end of the conversation.

It isn't. It's a great opportunity to go deeper on a sensitive yet necessary topic and to forge a strong connection. This is how you create a competitive edge by seeking to understand without an agenda. When you do this, you gain the trust and respect of your prospect. You learn their real worries and fears, and when you uncover the true objection, the "affordability" cover will naturally go away, and the door will open yet again for another conversation, another opportunity to engage you and this time, on a more sincere and genuine level because you've now earned the trust and respect of your prospect.

So be a little bold. Don't let prospects off the hook when they raise objections. Ask more questions. Listen with the intent to understand them. Create a safe environment for them to share their real concerns with you. Business does not happen between faceless corporate entities. It happens between genuine human beings when they connect and relate in a sincere way. The more human you can be, the more business success you will generate.

The Hidden: Unvoiced Objections

If you haven't heard a single objection or concern until the very end of your conversation, *and* the prospect doesn't want to go ahead with you, they have not been forthcoming. If they have turned you down, there is an objection on their mind that they haven't felt comfortable enough to share. You get to explore the territory for unvoiced objections now. Let's go where even fewer business owners dare to go!

Imagine this. You've been speaking to your prospect, Sarah, for a good forty-five minutes. She has been attentive, interested, and engaged. Then she says to you, "Thanks so much! This has been really great, but I'll need to think about it. I'll get back to you if I want to move forward."

No questions. No objections. You're eager to move to the next part of the conversation, and she's already closed the door. Your job now is to nudge it open and probe further.

You smile at Sarah and genuinely say, "You know, Sarah, I totally understand. I feel that our conversation has gone well, and I'm highly confident that I can serve you. Before we wrap, I noticed that you didn't ask me any questions or share any concerns, and when this happens, I get really curious. What, if anything, is on your mind that I can address before you go?"

The exact verbiage is up to you. The intent is this: to agree with her and then to invite objections while creating a safe environment for Sarah to share them with you.

If Sarah still holds back, saying something like, "Oh no! I just have to think about it! It's all good," it is okay to take yet another approach. You can say: "I understand, Sarah. Just want you to know that almost all my clients have questions or concerns before we agree to work together, and I welcome them all. Feel free to be transparent, as I'd like to earn your trust and fully understand your fears, frustrations, and desires for ideal outcomes. I want to reassure you that addressing any concerns is a necessary part of this process and my pleasure."

Sarah may still not open up to you. If she brushes you off nicely, let her go and wrap up. Your work is done here. You have invited objections and offered to address them. You have served Sarah powerfully and generously invested time and energy in her.

Keep Going Until You've Heard ALL Objections

As your fear of hearing objections begins to melt, you'll get more gutsy and you'll feel better about inviting more to the conversation. I see this happen with my clients. They go from being terrified of hearing a single objection to working up the courage to ask one question; then they listen with great interest. The discomfort is still strong, though, so after a single question, they want to rush past this part and move on to the next phase of the conversation. It's like they're saying to themselves, "OK great! We got that part covered. Check, check! Let's move on now."

My advice to them is tough and honest: Not so fast. That was a great start, but you're not finished yet!

You will make the sale so much more effortless if you slow down during this most awkward part of the conversation, which is completely against your logic. Your logic wants to sprint past any discomfort.

You must be thinking, "Is it not enough that we agreed to go through it? Now you want me to slow down and make it last longer?"

Exactly!

The message is in the discomfort: slow down to get through. When you rush, you miss the whole point, and you don't get the intended result. I've learned this lesson the very hard way in yoga.

I practice The Ashtanga Yoga Method, and my current nemesis is a deep backbend called Kapotasana, a pose that brings up tons of emotions and irrational fears. If you rush through the pose, you don't come anywhere close to achieving it. You must slow down your movements, be 100% present, control your mind with your breath, trust yourself to go beyond your edge, and engage all the right muscles while at the same time completely relaxing the rest. That is how you allow your body to expand and create enough space to achieve the pose. Anything else is a shortcut and a fail.

Still, one hundred Kapotasanas later, I am tempted to rush through it every time at first. Old patterns die hard. My irrational fear and discomfort still want to tip the scales away from joy and trust, but I catch myself. Awareness, dear reader, is the key to shifting those patterns and to stepping into the discomfort with trust.

The more you stay aware and slow down during the objections, the more space you create to allow the objections to come forth. Your prospect wants to empty all of their objections. Your job is to enable them to leave your conversation without a single unanswered question churning in their mind.

If you do this well, you will make their decision very easy, and you will naturally save yourself extra cycles of follow-through, wait-time, and additional conversations.

So, to make it super easy, let us use one of the best questions from *The Coaching Habit* by Michael Bungay Stanier: "What Else?"

These two words are easy to remember, and you can repeat them three or even four times, to ensure that your prospect has indeed shared *all* of their objections, even the ones they hadn't thought of until you asked for a second and third time.

How might that dialogue play out? See below as to what you can say after addressing each objection.

"John, thanks for sharing the concern about XYZ, which we just discussed. Tell me, **what else** is on your mind?"

"OK, great. **What else?** Let's make sure we've addressed everything."

"Good. **What else?** Anything at all that I can further explain for us?"

"Right. To make sure we've covered everything, **what else** may be on your mind as we explore working together?"

Naturally, after each question from John, you'll spend a few minutes addressing that before moving on to inquire further. Remember also that each time you ask the question you should allow the prospect to take their time. Learn to become comfortable with silence. This silence may be one second or fifteen seconds. Be silent and create space for them to confide in you, because rushing is the death of all sales opportunities. Slowing down is their savior. Train yourself to slow down not only in the asking and inviting part, but also in the listening and being fully present part.

Stanier talks about a commitment that speaks directly to this point in *The Coaching Habit*. He says, "Instead of going through the motions of looking like I'm actively listening, I will actually listen. And when I get distracted (which I will), I'll come back and start listening again."

The paradox greets us yet again: the more you slow down, the faster you get there—but there is logic there, too. When you slow down, you get it right the first time. You make rework irrelevant. You eliminate miscommunication from the equation. Hence, you become efficient and proficient at the task at hand. Plus, the energy you exude when you are in the present moment is a most attractive quality and a gift to anyone on your path in our rat race world today. Slowing down is a simple, powerful, subtle, and crucial skill to build for your long-term success.

Reasons Your Prospects May Not Share Their Objections

Let's look at some reasons why our prospect Sarah may hesitate to share her objections by putting ourselves in her shoes. Sarah is a professional. She cares about her reputation. She is inquiring about the services of a business that can help her with a challenge. She has the usual sets of worries and concerns that come with hiring a brand-new person to help her. She worries that if she shares her objections with you over the amount of investment or the length of the project or whatever is on her mind, you may react negatively in several ways:

- You may feel offended.
- You may judge her, i.e., think she is cheap and doesn't want to spend the money.
- You may feel you've wasted your time at her expense.
- You may get defensive and argue with her.
- The conversation may get awkward and uncomfortable.
- You don't have her best interest at heart and may say anything at this point to get the sale.

Can you see how important it is for you to create a safe space for Sarah to share her real concerns without fearing that she is being judged and measured in your eyes?

Do you see how you have to first earn her trust before she can open up to you? And can you see that if you are truly in service to Sarah, by following Mindset One—you are not selling, you are serving—that you will naturally do everything right and invite those unvoiced objections?

As you well know, Sarah isn't a rare case. Many prospects refuse to share their real objections, and many business owners don't know how to elicit them. Everyday, people leave conversations with unspoken concerns and unaddressed issues, and so much lost opportunity for both sides.

Why is this so common? Because we don't want to be either at the sending or the receiving end of any perceived rejection or judgment. In this case, Sarah fears being judged by you and you fear being rejected by her. You're both human beings; and you naturally want to be liked and approved. The risk of rejection and judgment is only in your heads, and yet its grasp is so strong that it can act as the dominant emotion behind your behaviors. So to be safe, by default, you both avoid the situation. In the absence of real communication and transparency here, no connection is made between you and Sarah. No real trust is formed. The objections go unanswered, and the opportunity fizzles out.

But It's Impossible for You to Be Rejected

You cannot be rejected if you are serving, and I'll prove it to you. Think about it: if you truly drop your agenda of "closing the client" or "getting the deal," if you are in the present moment and serving your prospect's highest interest, how can you possibly be rejected? The rejection happens the moment you make it about you. When you are serving, I'm sorry to say that it's all about your prospect. You should be too busy to think about your own feelings, and so it would be impossible for you to get rejected if none of this is about you.

In 2015, I had a rough patch in my coaching practice. I was working with a coach at the time and having a lot of Discovery Calls with prospects. I was not bringing on the best clients, and at one point, when a hot prospect turned me down, I lost it. This was at the heels of a string of "rejections," and boy, did I have a total meltdown! I remember picking a fight with my husband, crying, feeling angry and hurt and defeated. I felt so sorry for myself. I fully expected my coach to sympathize and take my side.

Instead, she calmly said, "Farnoosh, none of this is about you, so don't make it that way. It has nothing to do with you, so release that story. It will only make you suffer!"

And she was right. I suffered greatly through the made-up rejections, and I could see her point. It wasn't about me. I had not been rejected. What I had done, however, worked against me: Skipping over the hidden objections, taking the short-cut, rushing through the discomfort, missing out on great opportunities to create trust.

So go ahead, probe gently and politely to uncover all those unvoiced objections. It is safe and permissible and most definitely worth the effort. The more you know about your prospect, the more you can help them make the right decision. This level of care and attention is rare, and it is the best investment you can make today in your relationships and your future.

Good Objections Can Turn Into Great Business Advice

When we stay open, we can hear and respond to objections in an impartial tone of voice. When we remove all worries about getting rejected or judged, and therefore, have no need to defend and protect anything, we show up with total integrity and transparency. Sometimes, when we are able to really hear the objection, we may even be in for some free and unexpected business advice!

One of my past clients, let's call her Amanda, ran a popular online website with products for sale. Amanda was learning to be open to objections, so when one of her potential customers emailed her, complaining about the clunky payment system on her website, she was ready to act. She wanted to "overcome" the objection right away, but first, I had her examine this interesting piece of information: you see, Amanda had never tested her own payment gateway and checkout system, so we decided to heed the feedback, and we found out that indeed, her setup was not user-friendly. It was actually quite confusing. What an eye-opener! She quickly hired a new IT support person to set up a better system with an easier check-out experience for her customers. She thanked the prospect, who ended up buying the product after the website upgrade.

In reflection, Amanda wondered how many other potential-but-frustrated customers had reached that point in the checkout process and given up, and neither bought the product nor shared their feedback. This complaint turned out to be free and unexpected business advice that helped Amanda improve a blind spot in her business. What a win!

Learning to view every objection from an impartial perspective requires that you can not see your products or services as your baby. Objections are not about you. Therefore, they cannot possibly be a rejection of you. Or a judgment of you. Or a criticism of you. Objections are an opportunity to discover unexpected new insights about yourself, your business, and your prospects, so stay open in the face of all objections. You will go places very few business owners dare to go.

Now let us look at the common limiting beliefs around facing and addressing objections.

LIMITING BELIEF ONE: "IF I DON'T ADDRESS IT, IT WILL GO AWAY ON ITS OWN. IT WILL SORT ITSELF OUT."

How many times in life have you avoided issues, hoping they would go away on their own? Issues in your relationships at work and at home. Issues with friends or neighbors. Issues you may be dealing with in private and secretly wishing you could talk about. I know I have, a million times! We are so self-conscious about how we would come across that we keep quiet even if we would rather open up. We take the easy but low road of avoidance, rather than the more challenging but totally worthwhile high road of open, honest, and effective communication.

The thing is, issues do not go away on their own. Over time, they grow into bigger and thornier issues if left unaddressed. A favorite joke of mine: An elephant is on the therapist couch, and the elephant is saying, "Sometimes even if I stand in the middle of the room, no one acknowledges me."

We all do it; we ignore the big elephant in the room. It takes guts to upset the apple cart. It takes courage to speak up and probe when we hear a direct or implied objection to our offer. It takes confidence and compassion to set aside our own agenda—not to mention our pride—and to look the prospect in the eye and gently ask, "I'm curious, what makes you say that? Please, tell me more."

This is a very common limiting belief among entrepreneurs and founders with highly technical backgrounds such as engineering or product development. They are problem solvers by nature. They are focused on the mechanics of solving the prospect's issues, ideally in as rational, logical, and straightforward a way as possible. They are skilled at their work, and they are brilliant at what they do. But have them step outside of that known framework, and they lose their footing.

Take Bob, founder and principal engineer of his company. His prospect says to him, "I don't *feel* this solution will work for me," after Bob has clearly illustrated the proven statistics on said solution and his past success rate with clients. This prospect doesn't care about statistics or data until they feel they can trust Bob, until he can reassure them that he cares about their problem, that he can allay their worries, and that, no, he will most certainly *not* mess up like the last dude who spewed out similar statistics but didn't deliver.

If Bob wants this deal, showing more statistics and case studies (Bob's natural style) will neither address nor overcome the prospect's real objection. Bob needs to set aside his computer, tap into his empathy, make sincere eye contact, and find out what it will take for this individual to trust him. Bob needs to listen to their concerns, no matter how trivial, irrational, or illogical they sound to him. He needs to validate what he hears. He needs to earn trust and demonstrate care before he can educate and inform, and this is new and unfamiliar territory for Bob, who makes methodical decisions using facts and case studies, analysis and deduction, logic and statistics.

But as Bob pays attention and adapts his own natural style to the prospect, the awkwardness and discomfort begin to subside. He can see that there is no judgment or criticism of his work, so he relaxes. He is now focused on understanding and addressing the fears and worries of his prospect, however irrational they may be, because he gets it now. The prospect's concerns are important, no matter how trivial they may seem in his perspective.

The problem is that often we have a total misconception about what actually matters. What we care about isn't the same thing as what they care about. It does not matter if we please them or impress them. We need to *help* them, and we do that by serving. This requires that we show up honest, willing to tell them what they may not want to hear, and laser-focused on serving them and caring about them to the point of delight and, dare I say, astonishment.

Objections do not go away of their own accord. You can ignore them and be like every other business owner, *or* you can leverage them as your competitive advantage. Learn to address objections and you will forge a new level of trust and respect with your prospects, plus you'll help yourself be more at ease the next time you hear an objection. The more comfortable you can get about objections, the more confidence you will build in yourself and what you have to offer, and this confidence will come through in your future conversations.

Imagine what might happen if you come from a place of true service and go so far as to *astonish* your prospect with how much you care, how well you understand them, and how much value you can bring to their business, career, and life! You will begin to experience the world of effortless selling, because your services will start to sell themselves without you *doing* any "selling."

LIMITING BELIEF TWO: "IT'S NONE OF MY BUSINESS TO PROBE INTO THEIR BUDGET, THEIR REASONING, THEIR EXCUSES. IT'S IMPOLITE TO GO THERE."

THIS IS THE "ETIQUETTE story" that we tell ourselves because, well, who can argue with good manners?

You've had a great conversation with your prospect and you've been in true serving mode the whole time, and they even ask how to work with you, which you describe with great detail. Then there's a short pause before the prospect tells you that it's not possible for them to engage you in an official consulting capacity, but they certainly thank you for your time. A longer pause. You are torn, because on the one hand, you can't help but ask after their reasons, and on the other hand, your fear shows up masked as Mistress Etiquette. Is it even *polite* to ask questions and to probe further, or would that be the breach of some unspoken etiquette? You don't want to risk a future deal with this prospect, and so you play it safe. You nod in agreement and total understanding and ask them to reach out to you if they need anything. You know they won't, but it's the "right thing" to say. You go away wondering about their real objections, which you were too "polite" to find out.

This is a classic case of our fear telling us an alarming story. The source of our fear can vary from fear of embarrassment to fear of crossing an invisible line in the relationship to fear of offending or disrespecting our prospect.

We all know what fear feels like in our bodies, but that's not the only emotion present. What else might be present that may not be as loud as fear and yet just as powerful if you can recognize it? If you can slow yourself down and go back into the Seat of Awareness we touched on earlier, if you can pay attention with closed eyes and an ear turned inward, you will notice another energy, a quieter sense of wisdom in the background, your intuition. Which one wins is up to you, but it takes a little effort. Fear is louder than intuition, and it bullies until it gets our attention. We believe our fear's story without examination or inquiry. We take it at face value. That's why fear overpowers us so easily.

What if we paused and examined here? What if we didn't accept our fear story at face value? What if we said, "Wait a minute! How is it none of my business to probe about their objections when I am here to serve?"

To help you see that your fear is unfounded, let's switch places for a second. You are your prospect now. A potential business you are about to hire invested an hour listening to your challenges. They even offered you some great insights during the conversation. You told them in vague terms that you're not going to go with them. They said they respect your decision and still kindly asked your reasons. Would you think them rude or inappropriate for it? Or would you see it as a gesture of curiosity and a desire to better understand you and your needs?

I think you know the answer, which proves yet again that you would not be impolite to probe. You would be continuing to serve your prospect by seeking to understand them and help them arrive at a decision that is in their best interest. You cannot do that without knowing the real reason behind their objections. None of this can happen without a foundation of trust and transparency, and while that may not lead to immediate sales, it is the start of all good relationships.

How Does Fear Affect the Way You Show Up?

On an intellectual level, you know that fear is sabotaging your efforts and that being calm and centered is always far more effective. It's common sense, but how do you do it? Fear is irrational and persistent; you can't just brush it off as you would a nasty fly. (How we wish!)

Fear always affects how you show up. Instead of appearing confident and comfortable, you may appear anxious or have a funny energy about you without your being aware. So while you are doing your best in the course of the conversation, you may notice that the prospect is not totally at ease; they are not able to fully confide in you with their fears and frustrations. If this describes the energy behind your conversation, it's extremely hard to probe further when the prospect "shuts you down" with a firm objection.

The fear may persist, but if you can become *aware* of its presence, you can still take some useful action. See, the root of the problem here is your low confidence and low energy when it comes to objections, and this dip can send the wrong message to your prospect. You want to keep the energy of the conversation positive and confident at all times! Fear can persist all it wants. You just have to remember that you control your energy output.

When I asked my friend, Jason Goldberg, author of *Prison Break* and creator of *Playful Prosperity*, about the greatest lesson he has learned in offering his services to the world, he shared a mindset shift that revolutionized the way he shows up in his coaching business. In the past, he would have amazing coaching conversations with prospects and then propose how they could work together, after which the prospect would often decline or politely say, "I'll have to think about it," and he'd never hear from them again. The end result? People were not hiring him to be their coach.

He explained why: "I realized that I would have these amazing pure creative playful joyful enthusiastic conversations while coaching and when we got to the quote or proposal, my energy would dip. And whether we know it or not, if all of a sudden I drop my energy, what would the person on the other line feel? They may wonder if we are the right fit or if I believe in them as much as I did earlier. I was putting all this doubt in this person's head because I changed my energy."

So what can you do to quickly turn this around for yourself?

1. Watch your energy from start to finish: Your energy is infectious, for better or for worse! Be consistent with the level of energy you bring from the start to the end of the conversation. This relays your confidence in yourself as well as your ability to serve them in the highest way possible.
2. Recognize that a prospecting conversation is not separate from the proposal part: there is no separation. The proposal is a part of the overall conversation, in that it is an extension of how you can continue to serve this person and how you can help them create what they need.

In other words, Jason was truly serving the person in front of him at the highest level insofar as the coaching part of the interaction was concerned, and then, when it came to the "icky money part," he subconsciously stepped out of the serving mode as his own scarcity mindset took over. His energy would dip. The connection with the prospect would suffer. The magic would stop flowing. The prospect would walk away.

Remember: the serving never stops. The quote, the proposal, the offer—however you think of that part of the conversation—all exist 100% within the serving mode, and you must continue to show up with the same energy when you propose as when you were brilliantly sharing your art and craft a minute earlier.

Clarity can be your friend here. The clearer you are as to what needs to happen, the easier you can continue to either stay in serving mode or professionally end the conversation. To that point, Jason gave us the three points of clarity to look for with your prospects:

1. They have to understand what their real problem is.
2. They have to believe that you are capable of helping them.

3. They have to believe that they can be the kind of person to do what's required on their end in order to make transformation happen.

If you are not 100% clear on whether these three criteria have been met, it does not make sense for you to move forward to an offer, for it will surely be met with potential objection or flat out rejection (of the offer, not of you!). The clarity here is more for your own benefit as the expert with services or products to offer, not necessarily for the customer. The clearer you are on whether this is the right person to serve, the easier it will be to move to the next logical phase.

The One Word to Drop from All Conversations

When it comes to having an effective dialogue around objections, remember this: It's Not About You! Therefore, your statements should not be about you. Your aim is to help them understand the value of working with you or buying your product, and you need to do so in a way that it genuinely relates to them, not you or your company.

Of all the things you could be saying, refrain from these:

- "Here's what you can expect from working with me."
- "Here's what to expect from my staff."
- "Here is how we plan to meet (or exceed) your expectations."
- Or any variations of such phrases.

Commonplace as they may be, such phrases do not establish you as the ultimate professional on an equal footing with your prospect, because of the subtle meaning behind this one word. As you can guess, the word to ban is *expectation(s)* and all its forms and variations. The use of this word can be traced to countless miscommunication problems. You could argue that you're using it to show your commitment and dedication to the customer, and yet, as soon as you bring the word "expectation" into the conversation, you're trapped. In fact, Steve Chandler, who first caught my attention with his astute definition of expectation, calls them flat-out toxic!

Why is that? First, there is no *true* equality or understanding in any relationship which harbors the use of expectations. This breeds resentment, mild and unnoticeable as it may be. Think about it. If someone *expects* you to do something, does it not seem as if they have some sense of superiority over you? And when the situation is reversed, you over them? How do you feel when you are on either side—having expectations of others or living up to the expectations of others? It does not feel good because either way, you are powerless. Nobody looks forward to meeting expectations or getting their expectations met. This is not the way to nurture a healthy relationship between successful professionals.

Instead, use agreements. Come to mutual agreements. When you create agreements, both parties are on equal footing as they interact and come up with the appropriate arrangements. If either side has an issue, they simply bring it up now before they verbally agree to an outcome. Agreements are a powerful way to build trust and to cultivate new and existing relationships, and they get you out of that powerless modality of "expectations." Agreements are addictive and effective; once you start using them, you'll never revert to using expectations in your speech again.

Now let's change the earlier example and use "agreements" instead:

"Hey John [always use the person's name!], let's you and I now come to mutual agreement on what outcomes our working relationship will create."

When You Hear: "I'll Need to Think about It."

You can use agreements in any of your conversations. Another useful place is when you wrap up that initial call with your prospect and you hear the inevitable phrase, "I'll need to think about it." That's great, and we want to show our understanding, but we also need clarity as to what the next steps are. Often, we don't know what to say here, and so we wait for them to get back to us, wondering without knowing. Instead, come to agreements. Say something like:

"John, I totally respect that you need to think about it. When would you like to regroup? Can we agree on next Tuesday around two p.m.?"

If you can't get your prospect to agree on next steps to move forward, and if they are evasive or non-committal, go back to exploring the objections as we outlined earlier. Find out if there's something on their mind that you can address. Go the extra mile here, even if it's slightly uncomfortable. As long as you are kind and genuine and professional, it will come across as intended. Remember, you are doing this so that you get full clarity on where your prospect stands, and to do your part—the serving—fully and completely.

One invaluable skill my business coach taught me is to respect my time as well as theirs. When my prospect cannot commit to either a time to follow-up or a next step, if I've invested time and energy in them but they don't seem to appreciate that, or, worse, if I've had to reschedule a call for a no-show on their part, then I also need to draw a clear line. Here is a useful phrase that I've used countless times when someone has taken my time for granted:

"You know, Mandy, I really respect your time as well as mine. Our conversation is too important to rush and I feel now is not a good time for you. Can we agree on another time when you're able to be fully present?"

Agreements also tend to bring out the more honest side of people. For instance, if Mandy has no intention at all of moving forward with me and she was too nice to tell me up to this point, she's a lot more likely to speak up now, because it's a lot harder to agree on yet another time with no intention of moving forward. This is also when real objections may show up as she opens up to me.

"You know what, Farnoosh," she might say, "I don't feel like I'm ready to move forward and have another conversation."

At which point, I would say, "Thank you for telling me that, Mandy. I'm curious, what makes you say that?"

Never allow the conversation to end on a note of, "I'm going to think about it." If you've done your part, you've earned more by now. You've earned a mutual and clear agreement on next steps.

Striking a Balance: When to Pull the Plug

As you go deeper, you'll find that these conversations often reveal people's true character, and people will often surprise us pleasantly. But once in a while, you may find that someone is wasting your time and not even appreciating your insights or putting them into use. You may find that something is off about them, and it may just be a hunch, but it's enough of a message for you to know that deep down, you don't actually care to do business with them. You may have done everything, but they may still be unreliable, unprofessional, ungrateful, or any other character that rubs you the wrong way.

You have every prerogative to let them go. It is a sign of self-respect to draw this line firmly, and it happens to be a very different line for each of us. We each have our own tolerances and our own journey of growth, not to mention our unique intuition about people. The worst self-sabotage would be to neglect your own intuition.

When Pema Chodron, an American Tibetan Buddhist and author of several spiritual books, said, "Nothing ever goes away until it teaches us what we need to know," I feel she was talking directly to me. I was once apparently not learning my lesson in heeding my intuition until an ill-fated video call with a prospect. From the first minute, I had a strange vibe about him, but my ego wouldn't have any of it. "We're here and we're going to see if we can make a client out of him," I said to myself. After an hour of investing in him with my time and energy and coaching insights, he told me he had manipulated me all along; he had no intention of working with me and wanted to see what he could squeeze out of a free call. To make things even more awkward, remember, this was a video call. I froze from humiliation, mumbled something, and ended the call, and that is how I learned to never EVER betray my intuition.

May you be spared such a lesson!

Suffice it to say that if a prospect is getting on your last nerve, it's time to redirect your limited source of energy elsewhere. This is what it means to have our own boundaries as business owners and to serve those who are worthy of receiving our time, energy, expertise, and kindness in business. When you get the wrong vibe about someone, you don't need further proof. Cut the cord, pull the plug, walk away. Intuition never lies.

LIMITING BELIEF THREE: "IF THEY DON'T SAY ANYTHING, THEN THEY MUST NOT HAVE ANY QUESTIONS OR OBJECTIONS."

When I first started coaching, I was terrified of questions about affordability and credibility. You can imagine my relief at the end of those calls where the prospect "let me off the hook" and did not raise a single question. We politely danced around what I now know to be their unvoiced objections, and then I'd either not hear back from them or they would have a polite and ambivalent reason as to why they didn't wish to work with me, all of which I translated into a rejection of me.

My limiting belief was this: if they don't ask, they must not have any questions. Wrong! This limiting belief was selfish and short-sighted. It was all about me and my fear of being rejected or embarrassed if I didn't have a great answer to their questions or if I didn't have a response with which to impress them or make them like me. I was operating at the opposite of the spectrum from the serving mindset. When we are wrapped up in our own fears and insecurities, we can hardly serve. We forget that we are here to serve, not to impress.

Your ego wants you to play it safe because egos want to be right and liked and impressive. What if you took a risk here and allowed some discomfort by staying present and curious with your prospect? The unvoiced objections are the last frontier of prospecting; let them be your training ground. Be willing to get slightly uncomfortable so that your prospect can feel at ease and confide in you.

Unvoiced objections can teach us about other life challenges, too. We want to avoid the discomfort, which gives us momentary relief. Then we get the outcome we always get and we're unhappy, because it puts us back in our miserable comfort zone. Finally, one day, we get so sick of not having what we want that we find the courage to do what it takes to step outside this dreaded comfort zone. We do something uncomfortable and different, and suddenly we have a different experience, we can create a different outcome. That's where we need to go to establish a *real connection* with our prospects.

Now, what is the worst-case scenario of doing that? If your ego was right all along and your prospects have no objections whatsoever after you've probed, then you have clarity. You've been thorough and done your due diligence.

In my experience, when I started to invite questions and comments to the conversation, there was usually a pause at first, followed by the most insightful questions, which would have otherwise gone unasked. The more I slowed down in this part of the dialogue, the less I said and the more I listened, the more I learned about my prospect's actual fears and frustrations, doubts and dreams, and the natural skepticism that is present whenever we are deciding about a large investment.

One of the most unexpected insights to come out of my probing was when a prospect would tell me that it wasn't about the money or even my ability to help them—they simply didn't believe they were capable enough of making the change in their life, whether this was to elevate their business, raise their prices, move into a new market, or hire a new team to scale up the business. They didn't have enough faith that they could achieve what they wanted. They felt shackled to their old patterns. Now *that* is a real fear, which is extremely hard to admit, even to yourself.

If I felt I was still the right person to help them, I saw this as an unexpected gift, a chance to guide them in the right direction through mindset mastery right then and there, regardless of whether they turned into my client. The point is that our old patterns can keep us stuck and limit our possibilities.

What Would You Do in Their Place?

Whenever you wonder if you're taking the right step with your prospect, put yourself in their shoes. Some questions you can ask yourself would be:

1. How would I feel if I could confide my concerns about making an investment directly to the person selling it, without worrying about judgment or self-defense on their part?
2. What would I most want them to say to me?
3. What would be my response if they listened to me and really heard me and then shared from a place that helped me make the best decision?
4. How much would I trust this person when I can see that they are not there to manipulate me but to help me, not to trick me into parting with my money but to ease my challenge?
5. How would it further earn my trust if I could see that they would not even sell their services to me if they realized that they are not the best solution for me?

This act of probing about unvoiced objections alone can create an area of huge growth and development for you as a professional. Why? Because it gives you the ultimate practice you need to make serving your default mode in one fell swoop:

1. You step outside your comfort zone, quiet your ego, and call on courage and curiosity.
2. You make it all about the other person and come from a true place of service.

3. You create openness, safety, trust, and discuss real concerns without the usual filters.
4. You challenge yourself by learning how to properly address objections and you test your own confidence in the work that you do, the product that you sell, or the service that you offer to the world.
5. You do something that very few do in business, which is why I called it a competitive advantage, and you pave the way to delight and even astonishment for your prospects in the act of serving them.

As you may be beginning to see, the way of truly serving, not selling, completely changes the game.

GUIDING PRINCIPLE: DISCOVER THE GIFT IN EVERY OBJECTION

When you master handling objections with your prospects, you are a pro. Be persistent here and ensure your own follow-through. This is the least popular and the most dreaded stage of the conversation, even for established business owners. Your conditioned mind perceives objections as a rejection or criticism of you as an individual or of your business product and service. Even if you agree on an intellectual level with everything you've learned here in Mindset Five about objections, it is not until you *practice* the concepts repeatedly and apply them to your conversations that you can acquire the skill in your body and recondition your mind along the way. Learning to embrace an objection and seeing the gift in it is the best way to integrate the serving mindset and create a win-win outcome. However, that process may be met with some resistance.

How you feel about objections is directly related to how well you handle them. As you may recall from Mindset Five, an objection is not a rejection of you. In fact, an objection is essential to help you go to the next stage of a successful business relationship. You know also that you will benefit immensely by understanding objections on a deep level and learning to address them effectively. Even further, you know that inviting those unvoiced objections will start a powerful dialogue and put your prospect's mind at ease to share more. You know all this now. That's good. Now you need to *unlearn* the poor habits that get in the way of you applying all this, and for that, we will use the tools we've been building all along.

We established that you are able to change your mindset and grow into a new identity. We showed that you can write your narratives anew with a fresh script. We used examples that demonstrated the power of such changes. Now, as you do this, you'll realize that a change of this magnitude happens in imperceptible steps, not in leaps. You're not making small tweaks here; you are changing your entire operating system, and that's big. In this case, you are consciously changing your old habit of avoiding objections to the new habit of inviting them instead.

How might that look? You can tell yourself repeatedly before every call: "I am open and eager to hearing all objections." Write it on a sticky note and put it on your monitor. You can ask your spouse or life partner to remind you. Then, after you've had your first phone call or in-person meeting where you invited objections, regardless of how it went, celebrate this milestone. Mark it as progress and then refine the process as need be next time.

The fear is in your mind, and it's an illusion, as most fear often is. The only way through it is by raising your confidence. The only way to do that is to do the work again and again, to practice the new habits over and over, and to make the new habit second nature. Practice builds the foundation for new patterns, which is what you're doing here.

Rather than making the common mistake of most business owners who either shy away from objections or go into self-defense mode or just neglect to address them effectively, I teach my clients to do the opposite: to practice seeing every objection as a gift in disguise. Either you learn more about yourself, your processes, products, and services as they're being perceived by the person objecting about them, or about the fears and doubts of your target market, or about something else, entirely unexpected and new. Those are *all* gifts and can help you with business growth. There's so much value to the unexpected insights we glean in the experience of offering, serving, and receiving.

I'm going to pull inspiration from one of my favorite spiritual books here, because it applies. Michael Singer tells us over and over in his beautiful book *The Untethered Soul* to always stay open. Whatever challenge or anxiety or fear is coming our way, if we can stay open, we will receive the intended message from life and learn what we need from the circumstance before us. When we close up, as we often do, we retreat to our old selves. We think we're protecting ourselves, but really, we are holding ourselves back. In this process of serving, choose to stay open.

MINDSETS IN ACTION

GUIDING PRINCIPLE: YOU MUST DISMANTLE YOUR LIMITING BELIEFS AND START FRESH

LIMITING BELIEFS SURVIVE BEST in numbers. If you have one limiting belief, it's likely you have others. A single limiting belief has a tough time surviving alone, so your mind tends to attract other limiting beliefs to support the first one. Over time, you'll find yourself in a situation where you are glued to multiple limiting beliefs—facts and truths, as far as you're concerned—and you fiercely defend them if anyone were to even entertain an opposing view.

To create any positive change, you need to dismantle not one, but all of your limiting beliefs. They are roadblocks on your way, and removing one only gets you a little further down the road until you have to remove the next one. There is no compromise here, and yes, you do have the courage and dedication to retrain your mind and to set yourself free of the nagging voice of false stories in your head. It is a process, and once started, it picks up momentum. Once you have the awareness and momentum to dismantle the first limiting belief, usually the rest come tumbling down like a house of cards.

How Do You Charge for Empty Space?

Amy is my vulnerable champ here. Earlier, we talked about her identity crisis (Mindset Two), where she held on to the beliefs of her fixed identity from her engineering work while building her coaching practice. Fueled by the new identity breakthrough, Amy became aware of other limiting beliefs standing in her way. She found that she had serious hang-ups about money and getting reimbursed for her services, for example. "I used to let the 'money part' have the spotlight in every sales conversation, so even if I was feeling 'Well, of course I can help these people,' I'd counter that by saying, 'BUT we have to talk about the money part first!!!'"

The core work of serving the prospect took a backseat when she worked through the "money part" in her head. For instance, where it came to pricing her services, instead of focusing on how her services would bring value in helping a client meet objectives, Amy would be worried about calculating how much to charge and getting bogged down in logistics. In her past, Amy used to work on government contracts in engineering on space shuttle launches, for which she billed dollars for hours. She is your real rocket scientist-turned coach! In her intuitive and creative coaching work, not only was she stuck on what to charge for her hours, she was also stuck on how to justify her rates for the new type of work she now did, another limiting belief.

When Amy was an aerospace engineer, she worked with a concept called Net Habitable Volume, where they had to account for the empty space left inside the spacecraft for astronauts to live in. She laughs as she remembers how they had to draw up requirements around this empty space, this nothingness, and the challenge of justifying the concept to management, but everyone knew it was essential to make the Net Habitable Volume work. She realized that in a similar way, she holds empty space for a client in her coaching.

This empty space allows them to have breakthroughs or to experience a shift in their mindset or to see their challenges in a new light. Was she struggling to justify her value as she viewed it from this angle of intangible empty space? Yes, she believes. How should she price herself? What exactly was she charging for? Empty space?

Because she couldn't articulate the value of what she was offering, she'd be terrified of quoting anything, and she certainly couldn't imagine them paying for it. So her first limiting belief, the hang-up around the money, was now strengthened by this other related limiting belief, ambivalence around the value of her work and charging appropriately for it (Mindset Four).

During this time, Amy was still taking on some clients and charging okay fees, but she was doing so with discomfort and with borrowed faith and feigned confidence from the support groups around her, so her sales conversations were full of strife and terror. She may have had a set fee in mind, but she was far from convinced that her services were actually worth that much or, worse, that the prospect would even dream of paying that. She could bring herself to say the price, but if the prospect wanted a more in-depth dialogue around the topic, she would falter (Mindset Five). She was lacking the authentic confidence to effectively walk alongside the prospect at this stage of the conversation.

As a result of cumulative limiting beliefs and their consequence, Amy felt exhausted. These sales conversations drained all her energy as she constantly dealt with internal insecurities. Amy is also a fabulous mom and full-time homeschooler of her three small children, not to mention a frequent world traveler, so wasted energy was not an option.

Then it dawned on her. She helps her clients see *possibilities*, whereas before they saw *problems*. She helps them level-up themselves in skill and mindset. She started to see her work as expansive and infinite, well beyond dollars for hours. The "money part" that had been obscuring Amy's view suddenly became clearer. Yes, empty space was enabling this outcome as a tool in her toolbox, but her value went much beyond that.

As this happened, she no longer had to feign confidence or fear going into objections with her prospects. Her authentic confidence grew. The start of the turnaround was a deep knowledge in her bones that her services offer immense value and they are a perfect compensation for that value. As her limiting beliefs around money and value fell away, she began to see the big picture a lot more clearly.

How Caring and Trust Help You Close Big Business

As you become more aware of your limiting beliefs, you also become more aware of your unique gifts and talents. The awareness works in both ways.

Sales is all about relationships. Everyone seems to know this golden rule. It's common knowledge. But knowing is one thing; being and doing are each quite another. Are we really focused on every relationship in a real, genuine and authentic way? Are we putting our prospect's needs and desires above our own agenda every time?

This caring piece happened to be one of Amy's key strengths, but she wasn't aware of it until she became the CEO of renewable energy consulting startup muGrid Analytics. There, Amy came into contact with numerous tech start-ups and tech founders, and she was aghast at the utter lack of focus on relationships. It can be as bad as a total disregard to what the prospect needs; building relationships is only lip service, as these guys (and gals) prefer talking about their latest flashy techie innovation while assuming they know what is best for the prospect. Focusing on their prospect's actual needs wasn't half as exciting to these guys as demoing their latest technology with all its bells and whistles and convincing the prospect to buy it now.

Alas, that is the old-world model of selling. If you're reading this book, that model does not speak to you and it does not align to your values, and it didn't speak to Amy either. Even so, this hard push at selling is so ingrained in the sales culture that you may think building relationships is nice in theory but not in practice. Not so. You do not need to compromise on your values or your profits and, in fact, this can be your ultimate advantage over your hardcore selling-type competitors.

To this point, Amy shared an experience in which her company was bidding against a giant corporation to gain the business of a farm for a long-term contract. The big corporation could have easily won the business if it were not for Amy's competitive edge: cultivating the relationship first. "And it *wasn't even that hard*." she recalls.

Amy used her common sense and relationship 101 basics to win (yes, win!) the business. The questions she asked, which the big corporation blatantly overlooked in their rush to glorify their own product, were brilliantly simple. She divides her relationship-building strategy into two tiers: Tier One and Tier Two. Her Tier One Strategy focuses on these few simple, powerful, and open-ended questions below:

- Why are you doing this project/work?
- Why are you asking us for help?
- What about my business compelled you to reach out to me?
- What's the problem you are having?
- Why haven't you been able to move forward (on your own)?
- What's your end objective?
- Why is this solution important to your business?

Her Tier Two Strategy goes deeper by probing about what they really care about and what they *really* fear or feel frustrated about, what is the why behind the why, the reason behind the reason for their desire for help. Amy has seen the power of these questions so clearly that it's a no-brainer for her. One of her clients shared that they did not want to get pushed around by these larger companies (such as the giant company vying for the same business in a pushy, sleazy way) and how, more than anything, they needed an advocate on their side. What a revelation!

This revelation does not just accidentally show up in a casual conversation. You work your way here by building trust little by little, by asking well-thought-out questions and by listening and making your prospect feel heard and understood. Amy is applying Habit Five of Dr. Stephen Covey's *7 Habits of Highly Effective People*, "Seek First to Understand and then Be Understood," and the results speak for themselves, because even if you are selling a highly technical and complex solution, for you to rise above the competitors, you need to connect with your prospect on a human level first, which requires that you go deep and find out the real fears and frustrations behind the obvious "problem," and the real desires and dreams behind the obvious "solution."

If you can pick those nuggets of gold from your conversation, and go so far as to validate them with your prospect, using a simple dialogue such as, "Let me make sure I heard you correctly. You really care about being trusted in your marketplace and being respected by your customers, and you'd like an advocate on your side," you will be have created a huge competitive edge for yourself.

Develop the bond of trust and you can get some leeway other places. Example: your solution does not need to be the top solution in the marketplace and you do not need to have industry awards or massive brand awareness for them to hire you—you need to be really good, but no need to be #1 in your field. Connect on a human level, and if it's the right fit, you will have won the business, while showing up with integrity and putting relationships before business.

This, Amy explains, is how you truly put the money part in the backseat and let the serving take over, because if you do this well, the prospect will have already decided to hire you before you get to the "money part." Watching her rising success and joy, I'd say that Amy has truly achieved the serving mindset, and her limiting beliefs are simply a resulting part of her success story. Now it's your turn to start creating the same magic in your business.

THE MARKETING MYTH AND THE CONFIDENCE LADDER

For this section, I talked to my long-time mastermind friend and business colleague, Jen Gresham, whom I mentioned earlier. Jen and I have grown tremendously over the last several years and have pulled each other along on the fascinating journey of the success mindset. In our conversation, we pulled together many limiting beliefs, some that were already discussed in the book and others that are new, and we shared how these shifts have helped us level-up our businesses and can most definitely do the same for you.

I started by asking Jen what sales means to her. Her response: "To me, sales is just serving people, helping them solve their problems, but also opening up opportunities for them that they didn't even think were possible. We tend to talk about problem-solving a lot, but it's also opportunity creation, which is even more fun. Either someone wants help doing something or they don't, and if they don't, there is no sale to be had there. There are people who like help doing something or getting somewhere. Sales is simply the vehicle by which you help them."

When she started her business, she certainly didn't see it this way, and that she attributes to the emotional highs and lows that we have all experienced: You make some sales, you feel good about your business. You get a bunch of no responses, you feel bad about your business. In this way, you unconsciously attach your self-worth to your sales numbers.

But if you can remind yourself, "That person didn't want my help with this," you may begin to see the picture differently. Jen certainly agreed that we all need incoming revenue, yet even when our revenue is good, we can feel down when three or four people in a row have turned down our offer for help. You have to remember that their decline of your offer is not about you or your business. Your job is to keep serving and the right client will accept your offer.

Getting emotional about sales isn't useful, Jen continued, but if you can remove the emotional element from your lack of sales, then you can look at it in a useful way. "I'm either not getting a lot of sales because I'm not offering something that people want help with or I'm not reaching the right people who want help with this thing."

What's more, with the right business model, you need *very few sales*, which means you can afford a lot of no responses.

The Rewards May Not Be Immediate

This is one of the reasons people dismiss coaching: the rewards are not immediate or always tangible. Jen talks about this in her Money Mindset

Group Coaching program, in which she helps people shift their scarcity mindset, such as being able to have confidence to charge higher rates. The outcome of these shifts may not have been immediately noticeable in the six-month program, so it was easy for some of the students to get discouraged and think, "Oh this doesn't work," which is such a grossly limited perspective on how a mindset shift works.

It takes time for you to process a concept after you hear it for the first time or the first dozen times. You may know it on an informational level, but you haven't yet fully internalized the information into a deep truth, and until you fill this gap, you will be processing. You will be slowly discarding the old limiting beliefs as you begin to experiment with the new mindset shift, and this requires time and practice.

Jen has learned to put this out as a disclaimer upfront so that people come into her coaching with the right understanding. The progress may not show up in the time that you work with her, but if a year from now, you finally understand how to apply what you and she discussed then, you will be delighted!

How might this relate to your business in another industry other than coaching? Your offers lead to one or many outcomes, rewards, or benefits for your clients. Ask yourself: What are the rewards you create for your prospects and the time frame in which they can experience those results? Think about them in terms of short-term and long-term results, and be willing to articulate them with transparency to your prospects.

Confidence is not a Switch. Confidence is a Ladder.

Confidence isn't a light-switch; you are not in the dark one moment and then suddenly you find the switch and turn it on for good. Confidence is more like a ladder. It is progressive in nature, just like your shift in mindset and identity. There are many such ladders in your life, such as confidence in relationships, in taking care of your health, or in your career, and these ladders may be interrelated. You may gain a few rungs on one ladder and notice you've also gained one or two rungs on another.

Let's take the confidence ladder that applies to your business. You climb the first step when you start your business. Sometime later, you climb the second step; that may be putting your first product out in the market (yes, it takes confidence to do this!) or offering your initial service. Then, a while later, you may realize that you need to raise the bar in terms of how you run your business—maybe because your customers mistreat you or lack respect, for instance. So you manage to climb a few more rungs on this ladder and command higher prices and a certain working arrangement. You learn how to let go of the bad customers and realize that making money isn't the only thing you need in your business.

As you continue to climb the rungs of confidence on your ladder, your vision expands, your faith in yourself grows, your impact multiplies, and you start to associate with the higher echelons of business owners as well as attract world-class customers and clients. It may take years, even decades, to get to the top rung of the confidence ladder in your business. When you can see confidence in this way, you can appreciate where you are today and trust the process to take you to where you want to be down the road.

My brilliant friend Jen has raised her confidence to a level that she is not only making six-figure proposals to potential clients, but is also able to effectively communicate the value behind such a proposal. If you think it's easy to propose any number, I suggest you try it first. It takes tremendous confidence to be in total serving mode *and* be able to communicate a message such as, "In order for me to serve you for a year, it would be $125,000 for us to work together. How would you like to proceed?"

The shocking part about all this is that money wasn't an issue with her last prospect. He was honest enough to say, "Look, I can see the value of this, but I have a knot in my stomach because I realize that this is serious and if I say yes to you, I actually have to go and do what we're talking about, and that scares the hell out of me. It's a question of 'Am I really committed to go and really do this?'"

Even if your clients aren't going through personal transformations, fear and discomfort of commitment can show up in any place, and it's your job when serving to probe deeper about why someone wants to engage your services and, in the process, to uncover their real objections.

But the BIGGEST surprise in Jen's journey from charging a pittance for her coaching to now comfortably proposing six-figure proposals was something we've already discussed: Never ever assume who is willing to pay what. This truly is the biggest hurdle that gets in the way of sales. The myth happens when you think that if you start charging a certain amount, say, going from $1,000 to $10,000, you need a different "class" of people to pay those prices, because the current people you work with won't pay that, and it is an inner dialogue that you constantly need to call out.

I know that Jen and I both have had to grow out of this stubborn limiting mindset, and it is stubborn, alright, because it *almost* makes logical sense: if John is used to paying you $500 a month, and at the end of your first contract, you propose $2,500 a month, John won't pay that. Thankfully, the logic is very flawed here, and it all comes down to whether John sees the value of the new agreement and if he truly wants and needs that value from you in his business at this point in time. Naturally, a lot of that comes down to your ability to clearly probe deeper and then communicate that to John—as our own businesses and our coaching abilities have grown, Jen and I have charged dramatically higher prices, sometimes to the same clients, who had seen the value of the work and were glad to continue.

Can You Build Trust Fast?

As in any business, for someone to be willing to invest high dollars to work with you, I believe there must be in the foundation of your relationship a deep trust. I asked Jen if she agrees, and her response was yes, the trust has to be there, but—and this is an important point—it does not necessarily take a long time to build.

What does it take, then? I wondered. Her answer was simple: "Helping them! They have to experience or have a sense that they will experience deep transformation in some way."

She feels this can happen in as little as one conversation. In fact, that same day, one of her clients had sold his first $50,000 package in a single conversation, but it was a journey to get her client to this point. He refused to make any proposals, even though Jen had clearly outlined the rules of the game they were playing: Go make ridiculous proposals and get rejections. His reasons for shying away? He wanted to sort out all the imperfections of the proposal in his head before he made it. Wrong approach.

In fact, tying this back to confidence is key here. Jen was teaching her client that the only way to "perfect" your proposal is to have it out in the open and talk it over. Finally, he made a $50,000 proposal and was surprised to get a YES. Jen believes that if you have the right mindset, and are willing to hear a NO response, this process of making ridiculous proposals will help build your confidence.

Make Your Pricing Structure Scale

Now that you're ready to make proposals, how do you make your pricing structure scale? Let's say you have a current revenue goal of $10,000. If you are pricing your service package at, say, $1,000, and you talk to ten people, you'll need 100% yes responses in order to make $10,000. You cannot afford a single rejection. But if your service package is at $10,000, and you talk to ten people, you'll be able to afford up to a 90% failure rate and still make the same exact revenue, not to mention how the work will scale serving ten people versus serving one person. If this is prompting you to rethink your offerings, that's good. Larger packages always work in your favor.

When you understand the momentum and ease that you can generate in your business with a scalable pricing model, you will free yourself of the constant need to market, which brings us to the illusion of marketing. I cringe every time I hear a business owner say, "I need to market myself more! I need to get my name 'out there!'" Seriously, it's the worst fabricated lie about success and growth in business. No, you do NOT need to market yourself more. You need to learn how to serve the people right in front of you.

Don't Overdo the Marketing

When people struggle with business, they think their problem is marketing, so they go out and try to market more or take marketing courses or set up marketing campaigns, whereas what they really need to understand is sales. Jen put it best: "Entrepreneurs tend to overestimate the importance of marketing and underestimate the importance of sales."

You don't have to reach that many people. You need to understand what to do with the few people you have reached, and when you realize you don't have to reach large masses once you learn how to sell, you can relax and really be efficient and effective with your time, as well as present with the prospect right in front of you.

So remember: your problem is not marketing. Stop your worries around marketing and focus your efforts on sales through the art of serving. You have enough opportunities right in front of you to practice this now without an extra ounce of marketing.

DON'T LET THEM GIVE SERVING A BAD NAME

Bon Jovi. 1986. "You Give Love a Bad Name!" I lived in Turkey with my family when this song came out. We had emigrated there from Iran for a three-year stopover before heading to America, and I can still see the boys in the class singing the lyrics at the top of their lungs with their make-believe guitars.

What does this song have to do with serving and selling? Well, everything. You start with something good and sacred. Everyone believes in its essence. Then the shady and the unethical few get a hold of it and exploit it. They give it a bad name, whether it's love or selling, and now, the rest of us can't help but be cynical about it.

The abuse of the serving model is already happening in the marketing world, and it's a topic that came up with my friend Craig W. Hedge, a life coach and self-development author in Tasmania, Australia. I love that he challenged me on this when I first told him about my book—his skepticism on the topic of serving opened the door to a great conversation.

Craig said, "Many delude themselves and the people they are serving by lacking authenticity without demonstrated results and actions. Serving others has become a sales mantra for success, so the approach is more about how much money can I make under the guise of serving."

Craig and I have both experienced this firsthand from sleazy marketers and insecure entrepreneurs, and it's uncomfortable, to say the least, to be on the receiving side of fake service. So how do you spot those who are acting under the disguise of serving solely to meet their own agenda? Craig said, "It all gets down to demonstrated evidence. It's all very well to promise 'Oh, I'm going to add value to your life.' But where have you demonstrated that? Are you demonstrating that to me right now?"

First, we need to become aware of this behavior and detect it in others quickly. That will be the mirror that ensures we don't inadvertently fall into the same trap. Here are some indicators that need to be in place when you are experiencing true service:

- They serve you without an agenda
- They listen with sincerity in their voice
- They observe your body language and respond in kind
- They make easy eye contact
- They are genuinely interested in your problem
- There is congruence between what they say and do, the promise and the follow-through

Those who truly serve show you this evidence early on. Watch for it or lack thereof, and let your intuition be your compass here. Be wary of well-hidden tactics such as scarcity or playing upon your fears. Be double-wary of overstated credentials or status in the marketplace or knocking down a competitor to raise their own status. Your internal compass knows when someone is faking it. Rely on it to guide you.

Remember how we said that serving feels good, and that how you feel is a big indicator as to whether you are serving—which feels good—or selling, which feels not so good. When something feels off, it is off, and you *don't* need any more "proof" to walk away or end the interaction. Your intuition is never wrong. Give people the benefit of a doubt while at the same time holding them accountable to the promise of serving and helping under which they approached you. When someone offers to do that, look for the sincerity of the act from start to finish. Look for consistency in their behavior and actions throughout.

An example of this demonstrated evidence is how Craig and I met: Craig asked me to read one of his books. Being a top 500 Amazon reviewer, I receive a lot of such requests, but normally, I am *very* selective about books. I told Craig I was very busy and wouldn't be able to do it, but then I noticed he was based in Tasmania, where we happened to be visiting the following month. When Craig found out, he went out of his way to share hidden gems about Tasmania (or Tassie, as per the Aussies!) with us. He told me he had already ruled out what he was going to "get" from me, since I'd already turned down the book. He was serving me without any agenda.

On the receiving side, when I saw how generously Craig was sharing about Tassie and practically giving me a full itinerary from a local's perspective, I was delighted. That's when the force of reciprocity hit me; I read and reviewed his book in three days, knowing full well that Craig did not expect this in return. Rather, I wanted to give back. We decided to meet in Tassie, which we did, and a great relationship formed. That is demonstrated evidence, and it works when it's done right.

No matter how tainted something might be, whether we are talking about love or selling, you can embody the true essence of it and redefine what it means to serve. So it shouldn't matter how many fake marketers or indecent entrepreneurs use the pretext of serving to get what they want. It only matters how *you* go about it with your character, your intentions, and your approach. Your results will speak for themselves. I know that mine do every single day.

Let's give serving a really good name, shall we?

LOVE YOUR PROSPECTS REGARDLESS

Christina Canters, my star apprentice and client based in Melbourne, Australia, combined her background in architecture and her creative nature to build a communication and speaking enterprise. Christina has committed to loving herself and all her prospects, regardless of outcome. This kind perspective helps her show up with genuine presence, confidence, and positive energy, all of which make her even more attractive. In our conversation, she shared the insights that have transformed her business during our year of apprenticeship.

She summarized her changing views on sales powerfully: "I used to view sales as this thing I had to do in order to make money in my business and I would make it a lot about me. I thought I have to *prove* to this person that they should pay me money for 'this thing' I'm going to help them with. Now I see sales as an opportunity to get to know someone new, to learn about them and their challenges, and to explore whether I would fit into that scope."

Treating sales conversations as a true discovery call and learning opportunity is a massive mindset shift. Christina believes that regardless of outcome, she's learned something new in every conversation. She's either learned about her ideal client or more about her own ability to have effective conversations, such as how well she handled questions and objections or how much better she could do in the next conversation by improving. She is committed to the process, allowing the results to simply emerge.

One way Christina can see her own progress from her old mindset to her new way of thinking is when she's talking to her peers in similar professional services fields. She listens as they unconsciously use language that talks down their own value and worth, such as "Oh I'm *cheaper* than that coach, and it's a better deal to work with me," or "I'll just do this *little* thing for you and it will *just* be a couple of sessions."

To Christina, this is a huge turn-off, because in her new mindset, she can clearly *see* the value her peers offer as well as the lack of confidence and awareness on their part to present it as such and she encourages them to come from a place of love for themselves and their prospects.

What Not to Do. Ever.

Besides being a pro coach now, this mindset has also turned Christina into a highly selective consumer. Because she has learned to have powerful conversations and to be of total service when speaking to a potential client, she is looking to receive the same level of professionalism in return when she inquires about other people's services. In the past, this may not have bothered her; after all, the traditional selling approach, whether it's done well or poorly, is the norm in business, and funnily enough, she's experienced both sides of that coin recently:

Scenario One: Ambivalent Service Provider

She shared a story with me about a woman, let's call her Sue, whose program she was super excited to join. She'd been following Sue's brand for some time and was ready to jump at the chance of signing up for her program. But when Christina got on the phone with Sue, she was shocked at how the conversation unfolded—Sue asked nothing about Christina's goals or challenges or desires as to what she wishes to get out of the program; she jumped into logistics! Christina had to lead the call and ask questions that would nudge Sue to explain more about how Christina would get value from the program, which was still not successful. Christina's first thought was: "You've done nothing to learn about what I need! How do these program outlines even relate to my challenges?"

Despite the lack of leadership on Sue's part, Christina decided to think it over and have a second call, at which point the inconsistency in Sue's messages began to show up. Whereas she had first advised Christina to go for the one-on-one option in the program, she now advised her to go for the group option, without any explanation. These were confusing and inconsistent recommendations, costing Sue her credibility.

Needless to say, Christina didn't sign up for the program. She would've liked to share her concerns as feedback for Sue, but Sue hadn't even been curious enough to inquire about her decision. This blind spot of making it about yourself and seeing your potential customers as a replaceable commodity is a quick way to kill your business.

Christina summarized this experience succinctly: "How you conduct that initial conversation reflects what it would be like to work with you." If Sue had showed up the way Christina had hoped—curious about her challenges, interested in her as a person, clear and consistent about her own services, and as a leader in the conversation—Christina would be taking that program right now, despite her other dozen commitments.

When you adopt the mindset of serving, you will only seek to do business with those who hold themselves up to the standards of a pro, and you will require that others show up this way to serve you in a business partnership. Why? Because you wouldn't do any less for your own clients. Any less would not be acting with integrity to who you are and what you are about.

It doesn't matter how fancy your program, how beautiful your website, or how big your social media following; these are trivial matters when it comes to presenting a sincere interest in creating a connection, to caring and loving your prospect, to cultivating trust, and to being consistent in your message.

In this first experience above, Sue was simply unaware. She didn't know what she didn't know; she didn't know that she appeared ambivalent in her sales tactics and focused on herself with total disregard for Christina. This was an example of traditional selling done poorly.

Scenario Two: Pushy Service Provider

In another experience, Christina found herself on a call with a very pushy saleswoman, let's call her Brenda, who made assumptions about Christina's business, and who was practically forcing her program down her throat. Her first question to Christina, using a very direct tone of voice, was: "So, Christina, how would you like to be making half a million dollars?" Christina naturally found this to be presumptuous, where Brenda was simply assuming that she must be so far below this threshold already.

Brenda's program is built around teaching sales to business owners, of all things, and she was clearly demonstrating what she teaches in this conversation: pushy sales tactics. This call was such a turn-off that Christina told her flat-out that she was not interested. Again, the insights Christina has gained have shown her that she does not need to be pushy. In fact, quite the opposite is required to be successful, prosperous, and positive about her business.

It was clear that Brenda was a trained salesperson, following a script, using the old-world model of sales tactics to make her prospects feel terrible about their current state of affairs, which got them poised for the ultimate trap: that they needed her help. This model is the opposite of caring and loving your prospects. This is the opposite of serving.

Insights from an Entrepreneur Who Loves Her Prospects

Christina has developed a solid level of comfort and assertiveness with herself, her pricing, and her value, and so she's moved into a space of confidence with her prospects, regardless of outcomes. She put it this way: "Work on it from the inside-out and the outside-in. The inside-out is the self-worth piece, and you want to believe that you are worth what you are charging. The outside-in is how you come across when you speak it."

Christina connects the dots powerfully by adding: "I think it comes down to making it about the other person. This also applies to public speaking. People are terrified of public speaking because they make it all about themselves! Same with sales! This pressure absolutely cripples us, but if I turn it around and look at the opportunity of learning more about this person and appreciate that they've come to me already in the first place and then go about exploring how WE (not I) can best help them, I am back to serving." And that's what it's all about.

CONCLUSION

You Can't Hate Your Way to Prosperity

You know exercise is good for you. You've heard about the scientific proof behind it all your life and yet, you start and stop your exercise routines more often than you can count, and you're not alone; millions of well-intentioned health-conscious others do the same. I used to be one of them, starting a new exercise program with great enthusiasm and letting it go a few weeks or months later. Disciplined and driven as I am, no amount of motivation in the world could keep me in any gym longer than a few weeks.

Then I realized that the gym environment is a total turn-off to me. I find it nauseating. It does not matter how nice the equipment or how modern the technology, gyms aren't for me. So I had to figure out how to get the benefits of exercise *without* going to the gym. I had to find a way to love the process to sustain my regimen.

Fact: You cannot hate your way to results. It may work for a little while, but it's impossible to sustain. The negative energy will weigh you down, and why would you let that happen if there is always—ALWAYS—a better way? After a long ten-year exploratory journey through everything fitness-related, including kickboxing, aerobics, swimming, indoor cycling, PureBarre, Krav Maga, and every style of yoga, I fell into the Ashtanga Yoga System, which has been my personal haven since 2012.

Today, I have a strong daily home yoga practice. I get on my mat and breathe and move for two hours a day, six days a week. I've never been healthier or stronger or more flexible, and I haven't stepped inside a gym for almost a decade (except on my way to the hot tub on the other side, of course!). Beyond keeping me healthy, Ashtanga yoga has given me a strong spiritual practice, a sense of balance and grounding and inner peace, not to mention the best physical shape of my life.

I could go on, because when you find what works for you with exercise and health, you'll have arrived home. You belong with your process and you love it to no end. You'll have stumbled on a system that works for you and helps you achieve your desired goals. Who cares what's in vogue today or what everyone else is doing on Instagram?

When you find what works for you, you grow faithful to it. That's when the process becomes natural to maintain, and that's crucial, because it's with long-term sustainability that you build life habits.

The same applies to selling in your business. If you don't love and thoroughly enjoy your approach to sales, you are operating at less than your maximum capacity, you are missing out on too many possibilities, and you are likely not thrilled at the end of the day either. What would happen if you could create an approach that *invigorated* you instead of drained you? What outcomes could you bring about if you were *excited* about sales the way you are excited about your favorite part of the business?

Serving is a Win-Win Proposition. Always.

The linear approach to selling does not hold up when we are in serving mode. The linear approach tells us there is only a single win in a sales conversation: conversion of a prospect to a paying customer. The linear approach is black and white: you sell, you win; you don't sell, you lose. Incidentally, it is also all about you. Your "gains" or "losses" determine the success of the process.

Serving offers a multidimensional approach. When you come from a place of service and with a mindset to fully serve the prospect before you, you can *only* win. There is no losing. None. And there are many ways to win:

1. **Close Now:** You agree to work together now. You close the client.
2. **Close Later:** You agree to work together at a later date for reasons fully disclosed between you and the prospect.
3. **Down Sell:** You agree your premium services may not be a good fit, but your start-up product or your book is the next step for them now.
4. **Refer Out:** You agree they don't need your services or products based on what you uncovered in conversation together. You refer them to someone in your network who would be the best fit for them.
5. **Be Referred:** You agree it's not a good fit, and the prospect does not need a referral to another business, but they are grateful to you and will gladly refer others in their network your way.

As you can see, there are multiple wins in a serving conversation, but how do you do this in such a way that doesn't consume you? After all, you have limited time and energy, and you cannot possibly be of service to everyone who inquires about your help.

A framework with boundaries helps you make the right distinctions. This framework must make sense for your business model. For instance, I have a few books on Amazon. It makes no sense for me to spend time on the phone with potential customers for my $15 book. The effort does not scale, and my energy is better spent elsewhere. However, for my premium service of, say, a $25,000 coaching package, and for which I have a goal of perhaps five clients for the year, I invest generously in each of my potential clients. In fact, I'm willing to spend up to four hours (not at one time!) with a qualified prospect, and to refer to Jen Gresham's earlier point, I can afford up to a 90% rejection rate and it would still scale nicely in the end. Knowing this, I show up fully present and happy to serve the person right in front of me.

As you mentally scan your business model and examine your service offerings, think about what would be a sensible and scalable framework for you. The amount of time is not really the point here. Serving someone powerfully can take place in five minutes just as well as two hours! This is about the depth of the experience you create with your potential future customer, and with the right model, you will already be efficient in your framework, which frees you up to be right here, right now, fully present, and of complete service to your prospect, whether you spent five minutes or two hours with them.

Connect the Dots Forward

When you come from a place of serving, as Mindset One heartily suggests, and you are using referrals and introductions to attract interest, the first person you speak with may never become a customer or client. Say you ask this person to make an introduction to someone in their network and then you speak with them. They too may never become a customer or client. Now you are two degrees into an outer network, using the power of referrals and introductions, which is far better than cold calling, and yet no conversions, no sales. This is where you may start to falter.

After the third or fourth conversation in this manner, negativity can set in like a dark heavy cloud, making you feel so gloomy you may be tempted to take a shortcut by switching to rushed conversations and hard sells. For all you know, that fourth person referred to you by the third person may be your ideal client, and if you truly served all three up to this point, the fourth person will hear about it. The same level of service with this person might just give you your next client.

But if you get discouraged by the time you reach them, and either give up or have a perfunctory call without the real desire to serve, you will have sabotaged ALL your efforts to this point. The dots connect backwards, as Steve Jobs told us, and you can't know in advance how long it will take or whence your ideal clients will show up. You do not control that.

What you control is the process and your commitment to the process, and if you don't have 100% conviction that serving is the way to build your profitable business, at some point, sooner or later, you will give up. What needs to happen is for you to connect the dots forward with faith. If you believe in the process, and if your faith in serving is unshakable, you cannot fail. Your efforts will pay off. You can connect the dots forward with faith and trust and patience. So make a decision right now either to commit to serving or—I hate even to say it—not to bother.

This quote from *Rework*, a brilliant business book by Jason Fried and David Heinemeier Hansson, summarizes my point, albeit with some tough love: "You are not so special that everyone will pay attention to you overnight. Go for slow measured growth."

Your Great New Beginning

The end of a book that has resonated with you can be a great beginning to a new chapter in your life, and my hope is that with *The Serving Mindset*, that beginning will start with your new way of thinking.

The five mindsets in these pages are the foundation of that new thinking. You discovered that "You are not selling. You are serving!" in Mindset One, followed by "Enable your new identity to emerge" in Mindset Two. You moved on to "Care about your prospects and show it" in Mindset Three and "Charge appropriately for your services" in Mindset Four, and wrapped up with "Address voiced and unvoiced objections" in Mindset Five. You read stories, case studies, arguments, limiting beliefs and counter-beliefs, and you picked up guiding principles along the way to help empower and cement these new mindset ideas.

From these five mindsets, you learned how to think differently; you learned how to step outside of your current paradigm and see your situation—your business, your opportunities, your clients, and your prospects, as well as your own identity—from a fresh, new perspective.

As a consequence, in the future, you'll be able to take actions inspired by this new viewpoint in order to achieve your ideal results.

Now, as you begin integrating the five mindsets in your business, it is essential that you be careful, nimble, and flexible. Little by little, you can start integrating them into your daily habits, and I predict that, if you do so, you will not only create effortless success in your relationships with prospects, customers, clients and the rest of your eco-system, but that you will tap into the true joy and happiness that business ought to bring all of us. After all, why did we go into business for ourselves in the first place? To be of service, to make a difference, to have financial freedom, to do it our way, and to have some fun along the way.

The question to ask yourself on a daily basis, then, is this: How can The Serving Mindset be the central pillar in my business conversations today? (And by conversations, I mean conversations in-person and over the phone, as well as via any other means of digital interaction.) How can you integrate The Serving Mindset in all that you say and do in such a way that you consistently exude your desire of genuine service to all who cross your path in business and, by extension, in life?

This is the ultimate question for the savvy business owner with a desire to create a sustainable, profitable business. Mastering the five mindset shifts here is essential to achieving that goal, and now that you've arrived at this point, you are well-equipped to make it happen.

Sum It Up in Three Words

Sum Up Your Life in Three Words, said the poster staring me in the face in the sea of my social media feed. I decided to play. My three words came easily: "I married well." Then I wondered what I'd have said if the poster had said Sum Up Your Business in Three Words.

I'd want to answer: "I served well." I would want this answer to always be true and to rise above all other ways to summarize my life's work. That's how I'd like to be remembered, above all else.

This level of clarity makes it easy to know my #1 focus. Knowing your vision, in three words no less, gives you crystal clarity as to what you need to do right now. To be certain of your #1 priority makes it easy to always do what needs to be done.

And if you allow serving to rise to the surface, above all the other noise and minutia, you will pave the path to a prosperous business and a meaningful life worth remembering.

ACKNOWLEDGMENTS

It's a dream come true to have this book published and out in the world. As is true with all worthwhile dreams, many wonderful souls contributed to its success. And such is the case with *The Serving Mindset*, so I'd like to thank these kind individuals for their generous love, support, time, and energy.

First, I'd like to thank my husband, **Andy Brock**, without whom there would be no book. He was instrumental, from that initial meeting in the Toronto Underground where we came up with the idea, to keeping me motivated all along, reminding me why I'm writing this book, helping with every stage of planning, outlining, reading every early draft, giving me tough feedback I didn't want to hear, and helping us choose the right publisher.

Speaking of which, I am beyond grateful to **Skyhorse Publishing** for publishing our third book with them and being amazing to work with. First, I am most grateful to **Abigail Gehring** for saying yes to the book. Second, I am beyond indebted to my fantastic editor, **Oren Eades**. We could not have asked for a more patient, more thorough, more insightful, or more responsive editor. After the first week of working together, I felt at complete ease knowing this book was in the best hands, and I gladly followed Oren's advice with implicit trust and a grateful heart. Thank you, Oren, for making this book so good!

The conversations you read about in this book were essential to fully articulating our premise, and many helped with that. I want to start by thanking my dearest friend and mastermind peer, **Jen Gresham**, for always inspiring and challenging me, for exploring the serving mindset with me in our coaching practices over the years, and for sharing her stories in the interviews. I'm grateful to my two amazing apprentices, **Amy Simpkins** and **Christina Canters**, for going through my thirteen-month program and becoming such star clients by putting what they learned about serving into practice and seeing the fruits of their labor, and then sharing some of those stories here. I want to thank both my brothers, **Sina Bahram** and **Bobby Bahram**, for sharing the relevant parts of their experiences as successful entrepreneurs. I want to thank **Jason Goldberg** for being a unique motivational powerhouse and for sharing his wisdom on serving and for being super fun to work with, **Dominic Germana** for his fresh engineering perspective on running a business, my client **Anita Weber** for sharing the introvert expert's take on selling and her shifts with the serving mindset, **Greg Thomas** for his views on sales and technical teams from a manager's lens, **Leslie Crisci** for sharing her insights from working with successful CEOs with an aversion to sales, and **Craig Hedge** for meeting up in Tasmania over tea and challenging me on the cynicism around serving. I'd like to thank my role model and best-selling author of *The Coaching Habit*, **Michael Bungay Stanier**, for writing a generous foreword for the book.

I'd like to thank a few early adopters of *The Serving Mindset*: **Dan Sawyer**, **Patrick Reynolds**, **Joy Sutton**, **Jason Goldberg**, and **Molly Leavitt**.

I'd also like to thank those who read Advance Reading Copies of the book and provided blurbs: **Rich Litvin**, **Bernadette Logue**, **Dan Miller**, **Sharon Hill**, **Glen Oliveiro**, **Michael Knouse**, **Andres Valdes**, **Merrick Rosenberg**, **Leslie Crisci**, **James Halsey**, **Margalit Grunberger**, **Dominic Germana**, **Jeff Brown**, **Melody Fletcher**, **Caroline McGraw**, **Michael Knouse**, and **Sally Morgan**.

I want to thank my coaches, **Jennifer Hines** and **Bernadette Logue**, for helping me evolve into the coach and businesswoman that I am today, and for inspiring many ideas in this book. I'd also like to thank the coaches and teachers who inspired me from a distance: **Steve Chandler**, **Byron Katie**, **Michael A. Singer**, **Michael Bungay Stanier**, **Merrick Rosenberg**, **Eckhart Tolle**, **Steven Pressfield**, **Stephen King**, and **Simon Sinek**, to name the top few.

And I want to thank **both my fabulous clients—past and present—as well as all others with whom I've had a conversation** for teaching me more about the practical-world application of the serving mindset.

Last, but certainly not least, I want to thank **you**, **dear reader**, for whom I wrote the book. May you find The Serving Mindset to be the ultimate game changer in your business and may you reclaim your joy for doing the work you love without ever having to sell again!

ABOUT THE AUTHOR

© Emily Crowell Photography

Farnoosh Brock went from an electrical engineer and a project manager at a Fortune 100 company to a business coach, entrepreneur, and speaker in 2011 when she started her business, Prolific Living Inc. Today, she helps business owners, professionals, and leaders to choose their mindset, then to transform their world one powerful conversation at a time. She's also the author of *The Healthy Juicer's Bible* (2013) and *The Healthy Smoothie Bible* (2014), as well as *The Big Book of Healing Drinks* (2019). Find out more at www.farnooshbrock.com.